ADVENTURES IN THE WEST

ADVENTURES IN THE WEST

Henry Ross Halpin,
Fur Trader
and
Indian Agent

David R. Elliott
Foreword by Dr. Richard J. Preston

NATURAL HERITAGE BOOKS
A MEMBER OF THE DUNDURN GROUP
TORONTO

Copy-edited by Nigel Heseltine
Edited by Jane Gibson
Designed by Courtney Horner
Printed and bound in Canada by Webcom

Library and Archives Canada Cataloguing in Publication

Halpin, Henry, 1856-1930.
　　Adventures in the West : Henry Halpin, fur trader and Indian
agent / edited by David R. Elliott.

Includes bibliographical references and index.
ISBN 978-1-55002-803-4

　　1. Halpin, Henry, 1856-1930. 2. Northwest, Canadian--History--
1870-1905. 3. Indians of North America--Prairie Provinces--History--
19th century. 4. Fur traders--Canada--Biography. 5. Indian agents--
Canada--Biography. 6. Hudson's Bay Company--Biography. 7. Canada,
Western--Biography. I. Elliott, David Raymond, 1948- II. Title.

FC3217.1.H35A3 2008　　　　971.2'02092　　　　C2008-900711-5

1　2　3　4　5　　12　11　10　09　08

Conseil des Arts du Canada　**Canada Council for the Arts**

ONTARIO ARTS COUNCIL
CONSEIL DES ARTS DE L'ONTARIO

We acknowledge the support of **The Canada Council for the Arts** and the **Ontario Arts Council** for our publishing program. We also acknowledge the financial support of the **Government of Canada** through the **Book Publishing Industry Development Program** and **The Association for the Export of Canadian Books**, and the **Government of Ontario** through the **Ontario Book Publishers Tax Credit** program, and the **Ontario Media Development Corporation**.

Care has been taken to trace the ownership of copyright material used in this book. The author and the publisher welcome any information enabling them to rectify any references or credits in subsequent editions.

J. Kirk Howard, President

Printed and bound in Canada.
Printed on recycled paper.
www.dundurn.com

Published by Natural Heritage Books
A Member of The Dundurn Group

Photo Credits:
Front cover: top, Cree trappers. *Courtesy of the Glenbow Archives, NA–1041-8*; bottom left, Henry Ross Halpin *circa* 1872. *Courtesy of Flora (Halpin) Ross*; bottom right, Henry Ross Halpin, *circa* 1928. *Courtesy of the Saskatchewan Archives Board, R–B821.*
Back Cover: Flora and Henry Halpin with their baby. *Courtesy of Flora (Halpin) Ross.*
All maps are by Nancy Elliott, unless otherwise indicated.

Dundurn Press	Gazelle Book Services Limited	Dundurn Press
3 Church Street, Suite 500	White Cross Mills	2250 Military Road
Toronto, Ontario, Canada	High Town, Lancaster, England	Tonawanda, NY
M5E 1M2	LA1 4XS	U.S.A. 14150

TABLE OF CONTENTS

DEDICATED TO BILL BARLEE

*E*veryone's lives feature people who stimulated their intellectual formation. I wish to mention one who did that for me. In grade eight, at Penticton Junior High School, I, with reluctance, had to attend an art class taught by N.L. (Bill) Barlee. In his class I did not learn much about art, but he stimulated my interest in history. Barlee was an amateur archaeologist and superb storyteller. During art class he enthralled us with stories of treasure hunts, ghost towns, and Native lore. He even took us to the local First Nations reserve to look for arrowheads and taught us how to pan for gold. He himself had explored much of the back country of the interior of British Columbia, visiting many of the old mining camps. He built up an impressive collection of artifacts, which have been loaned to museums across the country.

Bill Barlee went on to be the co-host of a television show entitled *Gold Trails and Ghost Towns,* which is still seen on cable networks. Later, he entered politics and was British Columbia's minister of agriculture and food from 1991 to 1993 and minister of small business, culture, and tourism from 1993 to 1996. In 2000, he unsuccessfully ran against Stockwell Day for the federal seat representing Kootenay-Boundary-Okanagan.

The stories that Henry Ross Halpin had to tell about his life in the West would have thrilled Bill Barlee and if he could have, he would have put him on his television show. Thank you, Bill Barlee, for making the past real to me.

ACKNOWLEDGEMENTS

I owe much to the graduate seminar in Canadian economic history that I took from Professor Arthur J. Ray at the University of British Columbia in 1983. No matter what the topic of our weekly discussions, our conversations somehow always went back to the fur trade. The grounding that he gave me in fur trade history has stood me well in my teaching career and in developing my manuscript for this book.

The late retired Major John P. Elliott, my cousin, was an invaluable help as a research assistant. His internet research skills have brought to light many of the Halpin documents and newspaper articles that I otherwise would have missed.

Many institutions and people have helped make this project possible. Research help, photographs, and documents have been obtained from the Saskatchewan Archives Board, which has graciously granted reproduction rights, as did the Provincial Archives of Manitoba, the Hudson's Bay Company (HBC) Archives in Winnipeg, and the Glenbow-Alberta Archives in Calgary. Bill Russell, archivist at Library and Archives Canada (LAC) in Ottawa, was especially helpful in assisting me with the material from Indian Affairs that is held there. The Lambton County Archives, the London Public Library, and the University of Western Ontario were valuable sources of information on the Halpin family's life in Ontario.

I wish to thank my publisher and Barry L. Penhale and editor Jane

Gibson, who recognized the value of Halpin's story and arranged for its publication.

Photographs of the Halpin family were graciously provided by Flora Ross and Brian Halpin, grandchildren of Henry Ross Halpin. Finally, Nancy Elliott prepared the maps, provided encouragement, and spent hours checking the manuscript.

*D*r. David Elliott's edition of this fur trader's story is interesting to me for several reasons. One of them is the immediacy that most of us find in personal kinship. Henry Halpin was the husband of Elliott's great aunt, and David is the husband of my wife's double cousin. And David and I share an academic background with a strong common interest in the history of the northern Canadian fur trade. Now, to Henry Halpin:

A second reason that this book is interesting to me is that Halpin sounds like an echo of the youthful Robert M. Ballantyne, whose dozens of books extolling the romance of the northern Canadian fur trade were enormously popular in the 1870s and are credited with recruiting many youths into the service of the Hudson's Bay Company. Like Ballantyne, one generation previously, Halpin came from a middle-class family with an interest in publishing businesses, who signed on with the "Honourable Company" when the family fortunes were low. Also like Ballantyne, Halpin was a lacklustre employee whose business skills were minimal and whose real enthusiasm was for living among the Natives and experiencing the awe-inspiring solitudes of the great northern forest. In his elder age he still conveys his youthful sense of "being glad to be alone to watch nature in all [of] its pristine glory."

This is the third reason that I find this book interesting. We are given an image of a lifetime spent in the HBC's lower echelons. Unlike Ballantyne, who left the fur trade after his contract expired and became a successful author, Halpin stayed with the Company for many years, living close to many Cree and Chipewyan, developing a workable fluency in the Cree language, and enduring periodic physical privation with little hope for career improvement.

As a person, I find Henry likable. Of course, he could not be expected to present his life in terms that would convince us to not like him, but he does convince us that he developed good — even life-saving — relationships with some of the Cree he knew well. After his anxious time as a prisoner of the Cree during the Riel Rebellion, he spoke honourably in defence of Big Bear, a Cree chief, at his trial for treason-felony. This excitement was followed with an interlude of employment as an Indian agent, during which his income increased, and his marriage and family prospered. But then his wife's health became a chronic worry, his children multiplied, and his romanticism faded. It is a sadder but wiser Halpin whose reports to his superiors sound as if he has become very much the humble, plausible, very civil servant, and paternalistic benefactor of the reserve Natives he was employed to oversee.

His second marriage to his young and beautiful Métis housekeeper brought more children and perhaps a less anxious personal life. When the Hudson's Bay Company gives him his final termination, he becomes a farmer and "old timer," is finally more respected, a justice of the peace, and in a relatively secure lifestyle. At the end, he can tell us he had no regrets.

Good reading!

Dr. Richard J. Preston
Professor Emeritus of Anthropology, McMaster University

Author's Preface

*H*enry Ross Halpin (1854–1930) arrived in Fort Garry, Manitoba, in May 1872, a seventeen-year-old lad with an eagerness to learn everything he could about Canada's Native Peoples. That romanticism would be somewhat tempered by his occupation as an apprenticing postmaster with the Hudson's Bay Company.

Henry Halpin was a recent immigrant to Canada. He had been born in the parish of Ballingarry, County Limerick, Ireland, in July 1854, and came to Canada in 1864 with his parents and siblings. He was the son of Elizabeth Gaston Rogan and the Reverend William Henry Halpin, an Anglican priest who became one of the early professors of Huron College in London, Ontario, where he taught mathematics and classics. On his mother's side, Henry Ross Halpin was related to Bernard Rogan Ross who had been a chief trader with the Hudson's Bay Company and was a noted naturalist, and it was probably through that family connection that Henry was drawn into the fur trade.

Henry Halpin's employment in the fur trade took him from Fort Garry in Manitoba to York Factory on the shores of Hudson Bay, and across the prairies to British Columbia, northern Alberta, and into the Mackenzie Valley. During that time he acquired an intimate knowledge of most aspects of the local fur trade and a great deal about Native life, language, and culture.

Over the years, Halpin crossed paths with a number of important figures in the history of the West: Donald A. Smith (HBC, Canadian Pacific Railway), Big Bear (a Plains Cree chief), White Cap (a Sioux chief arrested during the Riel Rebellion), Piapot (a Cree chief who challenged the terms of Indian Treaty No. 4), Sam Steele (North West Mounted Police [NWMP]), Nicholas Flood Davin (MP and Regina journalist), A.E. Forget (lieutenant-governor of Sakatchewan), David Laird (lieutenant-governor of the North-West Territories), and Hayter Reed (Indian Affairs).

In 1885, while Halpin was working for the Hudson's Bay Company at Cold Lake in what is now northeast Alberta, rebel Cree took him captive (following the Frog Lake Massacre[1] during the Riel Rebellion), and he was held prisoner for a harrowing sixty-two days. Even in captivity he played a key role in that historical drama by becoming a "secretary" to Big Bear by writing letters to the North West Mounted Police on his behalf, which asked the police to retreat from Fort Pitt as he, even though he was the chief, could not control the angry young men of his band. Soon afterwards, Halpin joined the Department of Indian Affairs for whom he worked for the next sixteen years. After retiring from Indian Affairs, he returned to the Hudson's Bay Company.

Halpin began his career in the Hudson's Bay Company in 1872 at a time when that quasi-military two-hundred-year-old organization, its operation governed by military rules, including ranks, and its judicial function paramount in the northwest, was going through great transition. It had given up its position as the *de facto* government of the North-West Territories when it sold Rupert's Land to Canada (via the Crown) in 1869 and was quickly losing its commercial monopoly as the West became more settled and other fur traders began working the hinterland. Henry Halpin remained on the northern frontier of the fur trade, while HBC gradually transformed itself into a major urban department store catering to settlers on the prairies.

Halpin's career in the Hudson's Bay Company was hardly stellar; in fact, he appears to have been more interested in the adventures that the fur trade provided than in pursuing the business of the fur trade itself. As a result, he received poor performance ratings from his supervisors, and did not advance his career. That, which was the HBC's loss, has been our gain because his recording of his exploits in the wilderness of northern Manitoba and other areas of the northwest greatly increases our knowledge of the life of a fur trader.

Henry Ross Halpin, circa 1872.

Courtesy of Flora (Halpin) Ross

Some of the difficulty that Halpin experienced during his employment may have stemmed from his own attitudes of social superiority that stemmed from his ancestry. His great-grandfather, the Reverend Dr. John Greham, had been headmaster of the Portora Royal School at Enniskillen, County Fermanagh, in northern Ireland. The private school had been established in 1618 by King James I as a place to educate the sons of the Irish Protestant ascendancy. The school, often referred to as the "Eton of Ireland," included Oscar Wilde among its graduates.

Henry Halpin's great-grandfather, William Halpin, was listed as a "gentleman" in the records of Trinity College in Dublin. Henry's father had also been educated at the Portora Royal School before he attended Trinity College. He was ordained as a minister of the Church of Ireland, the Anglican state-church, and, for a time prior to coming to Canada, was headmaster of a private school in Youghal, County Cork.

Thus, Henry Ross Halpin had been raised in an atmosphere of privilege. In London, Ontario, he attended the Hellmuth College,[2] a private school for the sons of London's establishment. An early photograph taken before he left home exudes a sense of priggishness in his manner.

Although his education was limited to secondary schooling, Halpin had great powers of observation and an ability to describe in great detail the fur trade and Native lifestyle. He became fluent in Cree and had a working knowledge of several other Native languages. He could have been a great anthropologist or even a journalist. In fact, he virtually had ink flowing through his veins. His grandfather, Nicholas

15

John Halpin, had been the publisher of the *Dublin Mail* and was a Shakespearean scholar of note. His uncle, Charles B. Halpin, who used the pseudonym Miles O'Reilly, wrote for the *New York Times*, was an assistant-adjutant-general during the Civil War, and was a partner in another American newspaper with Teddy Roosevelt. Henry's brother Charles worked for the *Winnipeg Free Press* and the *Regina Leader*, and founded newspapers in Brandon, Calgary, Banff, and Black Diamond, south of Calgary. His sister was married to the editor of the *Calgary Herald*. Henry Halpin recorded his observations in two memoirs of his adventures, thus providing those insights into Native life and the social aspects of the fur trade that are missing in many other published accounts of the fur trade.

I discovered Henry Ross Halpin while doing my own family's history in 1999. I learned that my great-aunt Annie Elliott was Halpin's first wife. The 1886 marriage record indicated that he was an Indian agent. My cousin, retired Major John P. Elliott, with whom I was working on the family history, then discovered that Halpin had previously been with the Hudson's Bay Company. From the Saskatchewan Archives Board he obtained two incomplete manuscripts written by Halpin, one dealing with his life in the fur trade, the other pertaining to his captivity during the Riel Rebellion. Having studied the fur trade in Arthur Ray's graduate seminar on Canadian economic history at the University of British Columbia, and having taught Western Canadian history and courses on the fur trade for a number of years, I realized the historical importance of those documents.

Halpin's descriptions of the daily life of a fur trader are far superior in terms of social history to those written by Isaac Cowie, Henry John Moberly, Alexander Begg, and other employees of the Hudson's Bay Company. In particular, Halpin's account of breaking open beaver lodges, experiencing social life in the forts, and travelling by York boat and canoes is particularly descriptive and his renditions of Native lore are fascinating. Although the fur trade is now considered to be politically incorrect in some circles, it did represent the major economic basis of life in Western Canada before settlement and does need to be understood in its historical context.

What is presented in this book is an edited version of Halpin's longer handwritten manuscript that he prepared before 1928. The material was 121 pages long in raw form without title, chapters, or paragraph divisions. It appears to have been the first draft of a longer document that covered his entire career. This document is accompanied by a shorter sixteen-page typewritten account of his capture by the rebel Cree in 1885 from an earlier document.

We searched for longer versions of both manuscripts, but failed to turn up anything. However, the provenance of the documents has yielded interesting details as to how they reached the archives.

The typescript memoir of his captivity had been composed while Halpin worked in the Indian Affairs Office in Regina about 1894. He passed it on to a fellow clerk, J.R.C. Honeyman, who was to edit it for publication. The typed version is incomplete and has several gaps. Honeyman could not find a publisher for it and the manuscript was put away in an office drawer. Years later, when the office was being closed down, the manuscript was found, but Honeyman did not know where Halpin was at the time. In 1922, Honeyman was the librarian for the Regina Public Library. Believing Halpin to be dead,[3] he sent a copy to the Saskatchewan Archives Board. Another copy found its way to Hudson's Bay House and was later deposited in the Hudson's Bay Company Archives in Winnipeg.

The longer handwritten manuscript was given by Halpin to his friend Judge Harold A. Robson in Winnipeg on February 8, 1928. Robson made marginal notations on it. In 1930, the *Manitoba Free Press* published a chapter from it that dealt with Halpin's captivity in 1885, to celebrate the forty-fifth anniversary of that event. It was an abbreviated version of what he had written earlier, but does suggest that he had actually completed his memoir.[4] In 1932, the manuscript was passed to Leslie W. Garden, a journalist who was going to edit it for publication. Nothing materialized.

In 1945, Halpin's daughter Eva Lawrence searched for the manuscript. Judge Robson could not remember what had happened to it, but it eventually was found in Judge Robson's papers and given to the Saskatchewan Archives Board.

Because Halpin's own memoirs cover only a portion of his interesting life, I decided to augment them with other material he had written. Portions of the Oxford House Journal, the daily log of the fur trade post, which he wrote in 1875 and 1876, shed additional light on his personality and career in the fur trade, as do his supervisors' notes in Hudson's Bay Company correspondence. The Rebellion trial transcripts, when Halpin testified on behalf of Big Bear and against the rebels in 1885, give further details about his captivity, as does a newspaper account of a talk he gave in 1894.

It should be remembered that what Halpin has written about his experiences in the fur trade are his memories, written down when he was an older man, some fifty years after the events. It is possible that some of the material pertaining to 1872 came from a diary he might have kept. It should also be kept in mind that he has put forward his own version of events and his role in them.

As much as possible, Halpin's account of incidents has been checked against Hudson's Bay Company documents, such as trading post journals and Company correspondence. For the most part, his chronology of events fits the facts, except for the portions that deal with his time at God's Lake in northeast Manitoba and at York Factory. Editorial notations indicate where those portions have been rearranged into a more reasonable sequence. The accuracy of the smaller details rests on him. Overall, he has described his fur trade activities with a degree of gentlemanly self-importance. According to at least one of his supervisors, he often may have behaved that way, and that personal style could have been a cause of some of the conflict he experienced. His account, however, fails to mention those conflicts and they only appear in the post journals and correspondence.

Halpin appears to have been more candid in his captivity narrative. There have been a number of published accounts by those who were fellow prisoners with Halpin in 1885. Most have mentioned Halpin directly or indirectly.[5] The captives each had their own story to tell and each had varied experiences. As Sarah Carter, an historian at the University of Calgary, has pointed out, the published accounts of the two white women captives differed from their initial interviews after their release. Their later stories may have been embellished or truncated for personal, economic, and political reasons.[6] Halpin's court testimony in 1885 was more constrained than his 1894 talk in Regina, or at least, the newspaper reporter's account of his speech. His shorter manuscript may have, in fact, been prepared for that talk to a Regina youth group because he writes as if speaking to a Regina audience. So far, nothing was found in the writings of the other captives that would directly contradict Halpin's version of those events of 1885.

The years that Henry Halpin spent with Indian Affairs between 1885 and 1901 were also a period of great transition in Western Canada. First Nations people were now being treated as "children" by the Canadian government of the time, their economy radically altered and their lives proscribed by the Indian Act of 1876.[7] Although he had great empathy for Natives, Halpin was also part of the paternalistic white bureaucracy that tried to transform them from hunters and gatherers into farmers and ranchers.

Indian agents have had a reputation as notorious oppressors of Native Peoples, but Halpin appears to have been a benign administrator. His annual reports to the Department of Indian Affairs and his own correspondence provide a window into this little-explored occupation in Canadian history. It becomes apparent that he did not have an easy life as an Indian agent — a reality that created great hardship for his family.

While Halpin accepted the prevailing departmental philosophy of "civilization" and "Christianization" of the Natives, he appears to have had great compassion for them and clearly understood their objection to the hated residential schools. He even tried to have a local school established on the Moose Mountain Agency that he supervised, but to no avail, during his tenure there. When he left Indian Affairs, shortly after the death of his wife, Annie, it was at a time when the government of Canada was violating signed treaties and reducing the size of Indian reserves with the intent of selling off the land for settlement, thus preventing Natives from competing with white farmers and ranchers by restricting them to a subsistence economy. That duplicity began on the Moose Mountain in 1901 and may have been the reason why he left the Department of Indian Affairs.

I have reproduced portions of Halpin's annual reports to the Department of Indian Affairs as they illustrate his activities and thinking. No doubt there was some editing done to his reports before they were published in the *Sessional Papers* of the House of Commons. It was hoped that his original submissions could be checked against the published versions, but a search at the Library and Archives Canada failed it locate them and it appears that they were destroyed, seemingly by the Department of Indian Affairs, along with the daily log books for the Moose Mountain Reserve.

In this book, Henry Ross Halpin has been allowed to speak for himself as much as possible because he has a story to tell. Since most of his writing was in raw format, I have served as his copy editor, fixing sentence structure, and adding necessary words to clarify the text, but sparingly retained some of his usage of the language of the time, such as "Indian" and "Halfbreed": He would not have meant any disrespect by such terms. Almost all the children born to Hudson's Bay Company fur traders were of mixed parentage as HBC employees could not bring white wives with them from England and Scotland until very late in the Company's history. Some people of mixed race (the Métis) who had lived with their Native mothers (the women who became known as "country wives") spoke the European languages of their fathers, but identified themselves according to the Native origin of their mothers — Cree, Sioux, et cetera and so forth. Fur traders tended to prefer mixed-race women as spouses because they could bridge the two cultures. There were French-speaking Métis and English-speaking Métis (mostly with roots in the Orkney Islands of Scotland), each group having its own separate and distinct society in Western Canada. In his use of the term *Halfbreed*, Halpin rarely makes the distinction between the two societies, only occasionally noting the origin as French. Thus, in substituting the term *Métis* in the text it is not always clear, except for his occasional reference to origin, which has been maintained, whether the reference is to the English-speaking or French-speaking. Interestingly, his second wife Flora was of Scottish-Native origin. Unfortunately, his story is incomplete for the period covered between the two manuscripts and after the second one. For the silent years, I have provided transitional and contextual chapters, using primary sources and quotations from them. The Imperial measurements in use at the time; mile, foot, yard, and so forth have been left intact.

Because this book is intended for a general readership, and because I wish to maintain the narrative form that he employed, I avoided the temptation to create a book of historical documents. Keeping in mind Donald Creighton's dictum that "history should be literature," I have presented the material in this fashion to remain faithful to Halpin's original narrative intent, otherwise the final product could be as dry as Harold A. Innis's *Fur Trade in Canada,* frequently criticized for its tone and lack of social history.

Enjoy Halpin's *Adventures in the West.*

David R. Elliott, PhD
Parkhill, Ontario

1 Fort Garry

I have been asked by a friend of mine to write an account of my life in Manitoba, the North-West Territories, and British Columbia, which covers a period of more than fifty years. I find it very hard for me to decide what would or would not be of interest to him or others because events that were of much moment to me in those far back days may be little thought of now. However, I am going to write an account of how the country and its people looked from my point of view. I am going to "hew to the line and let the chips fall where they may."

I arrived at Fort Garry, what is now the City of Winnipeg, on a very wet Saturday afternoon, at the end of the month of May 1872. I was already articling as an "apprentice clerk" in the service of the Honourable Hudson's Bay Company, so I did not have to look around for a "job."[1]

I took my letter of introduction to the officer in charge of Fort Garry. I was then given accommodation in the officers' quarters and found myself in a very comfortable position. I had the pleasure of meeting some very fine men belonging to the service at Fort Garry and others from some of the northern posts. Many of these men were old employees of the Company and I enjoyed my first night with them very much, listening to stories of life at the outposts of the Company in "the great lone land" and I wished from the bottom of my heart that I could go home with any one of these "Factors" and enjoy the life they were leading, and take part in the stirring events narrated by some of them. I have found out since

Courtesy of the Glenbow Archives, NA–249–11

Steamer Dakota *at the mouth of the Assiniboine River, 1872, with Upper Fort Garry in background. Until the completion of the Canadian Pacific Railway in 1885, transportation in the West was primarily by its waterways. Goods from central Canada came via steamship on the Red River from Grand Forks, North Dakota.*

that many of these "events" were manufactured out of whole cloth for my special benefit. However, they meant well and since then I have at various times helped to make a youngster feel the thrill of the West with the same kind of tales.

Many years of my life had been spent in Ireland where I had seen many forts and much fortification. Fort Garry did not seem to me to be anything like the forts I had seen in Ireland, but still the walls were high enough and strong enough, I thought, to keep out the Natives, if they happened to act ugly. But so far as I could learn, the Fort had never been attacked by Indians since it was built. And that first night in Fort Garry I should have been delighted if all them in the country had laid siege to it and given me a chance to show what an Irishman could do. (The people in the Fort were mostly Scottish, which I suppose accounts for wishing to show my valour.)

A year or two before my time [1870], this same Fort Garry had been taken by French Métis, with Louis Riel at their head, but at that time there was no fighting. They simply walked in at the gate and took charge, and so far as I can learn, did not molest any of the Hudson's Bay Company's people, though they did, I believe, help themselves to provisions and other things from the stores, and from what I was told at that time, it seems to me that the Hudson's Bay Company's people did nothing to prevent these Halfbreed rebels from doing what they liked, and it has since been said that the Company was to blame for the uprising.

The day after my arrival at Fort Garry, being Sunday, I went up to the village to visit an old school fellow of mine who was running a general store in partnership with a gentleman named Wilson. The firm went under the name of Wilson and Hyman. Walter Hyman was a brother of C.W. Hyman, who held a cabinet position in the Laurier government for some years, and is, I think, still a resident of London, Ontario.

I had a good long chat with Walter and then went out for a look around the town or "City," as Walt called it. Hyman's Store stood, as I remember, on the prairie, somewhere near where the Corona Hotel now stands, and I remember I had to cross a mudhole on a plank to get to the store's door.

After I had walked to what is now the corner of Portage Avenue and Main Street, I walked out onto what people called the Portage Road, and when I had gone about a mile, I saw to my right a large number of Indian lodges. They were quite a distance away, but I was determined to visit them, so off I started across the prairie. I had to walk about another mile or more before I came to the outskirts of the camp. There must have been in the

Courtesy of the Glenbow Archives, NA-2536–22

View of Winnipeg, circa *1871.*

neighbourhood of three hundred lodges and tents. I did not know whether I would be welcome in the camp or not but was going to find out anyway.

There were lots of half-clothed children playing on the prairie land between the lodges, and, as they did not seem to mind my being there, I took it for granted that they had seen white people before and felt no alarm. While standing looking at the children, I heard a drum and started off in the direction from which the sound came, and in a few minutes I was in the middle of at least a hundred Native people.

These were the first "Blanket Indians"[2] I had been close to. I had seen a few before when passing through Minnesota, but was now right among them. There was a big dance of some sort under way and all the men were painted in great style; their faces were painted in stripes of red and blue and their breasts either green or yellow. There were many Métis in the camp and the one I met who could speak good English told me that the Indians were of the Sioux tribe from Portage La Prairie and that some also were from the United States on a visit to their Canadian friends.

Hamelin was my new-found friend's name.[3] He told me he had just got back from the buffalo hunt far away on the plains near Medicine Hat. He invited me to his camp and asked me to eat, which I was quite willing to do. So down we sat, while his two pretty daughters prepared a good meal, consisting of dried and smoked buffalo tongues, and dried meat from the choice parts of the buffalo. The vegetable on the "menu" consisted of "Hard Tack" or sea biscuits fried in marrow fat, after being soaked in hot water. There was a bottle of HBC rum on hand, but the principal beverage was black tea, with lots of sugar but no milk. I enjoyed my dinner and my surroundings, and went back to the Fort, with my mind made up to get as far north or west as I could, so long as I would be near, if not living with, Indians.

Friend Hamelin called on me at the Fort in a day or so, and I did the honours of my room, in the shape of a good glass of rum and a smoke. I also sent a present to Hamelin's daughters — two silk handkerchiefs which I had brought from home [London, Ontario] with me.

The world is small. I met Hamelin twice after he returned to the plains, once at Swift Current, Saskatchewan, where I went to trade for buffalo robes. This was in 1877 and the next time was at Lac La Biche in

1880 where he had settled down and kept a store and was doing well.[4]

When Hamelin visited me at the Fort, he said he was leaving for the West in a few more days and said he would be glad if I could come and see him again before he left and that he would take me all over the camp and show me all that was to be seen. I was glad to accept his invitation, and a day or so later I asked permission of Mr. [John H.] McTavish, the officer in charge of Fort Garry, to visit the Indian camp. He kindly consented to my doing so and advised me not to fall too deeply in love with any of the "prairie flowers," which I promised not to do. I was only seventeen years of age, or I should not have been so ready with my promises.

Courtesy of the Glenbow Archives, NA–2069–4

Cree teepees and Red River cart.

I did not have to walk to the camp this time because I was able to borrow one of the Hudson's Bay Company ponies, a large herd of which were "rounded up" each day near the Fort. These ponies were used with the "Red River carts" for freighting the Company's supplies to the "far west" and were hardy little animals.

I put a saddle on my pony and started up the "River Road," which is now Main Street, on my way to the camp. When I got to the turn at "Portage Road" I noticed quite a crowd of men and boys. Many Indians were to be seen and from the way they acted and also the noise they made, I was sure something out of the common was afoot. When I got closer and could see over the heads of the party, which I could do being on horseback, I saw that a fight was on. One of the fighters, I could see, was a soldier, and the other a big fellow with a red face, with an even redder handkerchief tied round his neck, and long boots. His broad-brimmed hat was on the ground, not far from where he lay — he having been just "knocked out" by the soldier. Poor fellow. He was a typical cowboy. He could fight, I guess, rough and tumble, but the trained soldier, though much smaller and slighter, knew how to use his fists. I waited to see the finish of the fight, which was not long, and it ended as usual, in those happy and free days, with the principals shaking hands, and an adjournment to the bar to "liquor up."

I met and was introduced to the soldier later on. He was a decent sort of chap. He had lived in Winnipeg for many years and was married to one of Winnipeg's nicest girls. The poor fellow died some years ago in the States, and I do not know what became of his wife. I don't think there were children by the marriage.

I arrived at the Indian camp and was welcomed by my friend Hamelin. My pony was tied to a picket rope and left to graze, while I went off with Hamelin to see the surroundings, and perhaps, get acquainted with some of the Indian men. Being an employee of the Hudson's Bay Company helped to make you friends in those days and some of the local Natives gave a different reception to Company people than what they gave to a Canadian, no matter what his position was.

Riches did not count with the Native Peoples. If a Canadian came to the camp and displayed his money or good clothes, the Indians put him down as a "crook" and kept him at a distance. They thought he was trying to take advantage of them in some way.

There were two or three different tribes represented in the camp — Sioux, Salteaux, Cree of the Plains, and "Swampy Cree" from down the Red River. The first tent we visited belonged to one of the head men of the Peguis Band, who were living where the town of Selkirk now stands. He could speak a little English, and when I mentioned my uncle Bernard Ross, chief factor of the HBC, I was given the "freedom of the camp," so to speak. My uncle had been in charge of Lower Fort Garry and they were old friends. As usual I was invited to eat, but as it was not long since I had eaten, I had to decline.

The next tent visited was that of the Sioux chief "White Cap." He was, he said, pleased at my visit, but as Hamelin could not speak Sioux we did not stay long. Thirteen years after that, in 1885, I met White Cap at his reserve near Fort Qu'Appelle and he said he remembered my visit to him along with Hamelin in 1872.

I had dealings with White Cap later on, when I was at Muscowpetung Reserve, east of Regina in the Qu' Appelle Valley, and I always found him easy to please and willing to do as the government wished, but like all the "Old Time" Indians he hated being on a reserve and was forever asking for "permits"[5] to visit friends in other parts of the country.

I also visited some of Hamelin's friends and found them a fine class of people, but as I could not speak French, and most of them very little English, we made very little headway. However, in the tent of a man named Xavier La Londre, the invitation to dinner could not be overcome, so Hamelin and I sat down to the usual camp dainties and did full justice to them.

The descendants of many of the people I met that afternoon are now living in St. Boniface and other places along the Red River, and many more are living along the South Branch of the Saskatchewan River near Duck Lake. I think they are a commendable group of people and no dishonour to the race from which they sprang on either side.

It was getting dark when I turned my pony homewards and I had the misfortune to get lost on my way back. My pony wandered down a bush trail without my knowing it and I was wandering in the bush on the "flats" below where the Union Depot in Winnipeg now stands. I was lost

Courtesy of the Glenbow Archives, NA–1940–3

White Cap, Sioux chief, as he looked in 1885. White Cap was arrested for treason during the Northwest Rebellion, but was later acquitted.

for an hour and did not find my way to the Fort until after I had landed at the corner of Portage Road. I might have been out all night, but for the fact that I heard a band playing. I headed my pony towards the sound and after fifteen or twenty minutes I came out of the bush somewhere near where the CNR [Canadian National Railway] freight sheds now stand. It was after twelve o'clock when I arrived home. No one asked any questions and I did not feel like telling that I had been lost, and so the matter dropped. I soon went to bed, tired and happy, to dream of buffalo hunting and Indians, and, I may as well tell the truth, of a dozen at least, lovely dark-eyed "French" Métis maidens.

The pictures one sees from time to time in the newspapers and magazines give one a fair idea of what the exterior of Fort Garry looked like in the early days, but I have not seen or read anything of the interior, so I am going to give you, as well as I can remember, a word picture of the inside of the Fort. In the middle of the square stood the guard room, or officers' quarters, a large two-storey building. It was built of logs and thickly plastered on the outside. The lower part was used as offices for the officer in charge and also for the dozen or more clerks employed in the Company's business. It was the head office for the district and a very busy place in summer when the brigades of boats from the North and freighters from the West arrived, bringing in their thousands of packs of buffalo robes and furs, which were then shipped to Montreal and from there to London, England.

Inside Upper Fort Garry. The buildings on the right are warehouses. The main office with officers' quarters above is the building with the exterior staircase in the left foreground.

Fort Garry was a bustling place in those days. The boatmen, some from as far away as Rocky Mountain House on the North Branch of the Saskatchewan River, about two hundred miles west of Edmonton, had to be made ready for the return to the various inland posts from which they came, loaded with supplies for the coming year. The "outfits" [supplies] for the different posts had been packed during the winter, requisitions having been received at Fort Garry either by the December or March packets [fur shipments] from these distant posts, and some had been forwarded the previous summer from distant places in the McKenzie and Athabasca districts, some of these posts being far inside the Arctic Circle. Little time was lost in getting the men started on their homeward trip as every day counted and even then there was a chance of some of the boats being frozen in before reaching their destinations.

The packs that were being sent to the interior by boat, with the exception of those posts on Lake Winnipeg, were packed to weigh about eighty pounds as they had to be carried over hundreds of portages by the boatmen before they got them home. Some of the portages were a mile long, but the average length, say, between Fort Garry and Nelson River Post, would be about a hundred yards, many of them so steep that a block and tackle had to be used to get the boats up the hill and then let them down slowly on the other side.

These boatmen, or "voyageurs" as we called them, were a hardy lot. Most of them were small, slightly built men, a mass of bone and sinew. I don't think I ever saw what one could call a fat carrier that was any good. I have seen a man, that I do not think could have weighed more than a hundred and twenty-five or thirty pounds and not more than five feet two or three in height, take three eighty-pound packs on his back and start off on a trotting race over a mile-long portage. The first pack was tied with a portage strap and lifted by the man himself and placed as he wished it on his back with the broad part of the strap just above his forehead. The balance of the load was put on by a man left at the end of the portage for that purpose.

There was great rivalry among the men of the different posts as to which one had the best carriers, and each post had its fancy man and they would bet all they had in the way of tobacco and clothing on their champion. At times the trial of strength and swiftness would start a quarrel and more than once I have been the spectator of a something like the proverbial "Donnybrook Fair," but if anyone was hurt so that he could not work, his companions turned in and did his share.

I once saw one of these small-sized packers stand up under a seven-hundred-pound load of shot and I believe he could have stood more had not the portage strap broken. Of course he was not supposed to carry this. It was only a test of strength.

I shall now return to my subject with regard to the interior of Fort Garry. To reach the officers' quarters above the office, one had to use a stairs on the outside of the building. There were, I think, eight or more bedrooms and a large sitting room. The place was very comfortable and home-like and the officers using the bedrooms had fixed them up to their own taste. The furniture was all homemade, the product of the fort carpenter, and was made for strength more than beauty. A big "Carson" stove stood in the middle of the sitting room and it must have been a comfortable place to put in time in winter when the duties of the day were over.

There was a splendid library in the office downstairs full of books that even at that time were hard to get and at present it would be almost impossible to find one of them. There were books (first editions) by men like Sir George Simpson [governor of the Hudson's Bay Company], Samuel Hearne [HBC explorer (1745–92)], R.M. Ballantyne [HBC clerk at York Factory in the 1840s], and other mighty men who had at one time or another been connected with the Honourable Company of Gentlemen Adventurers [the original name of the Hudson's Bay Company] trading into Hudson Bay. Many a night the sun was getting near the horizon ere I would close my book to try and get an hour's sleep before I had to get up, eat my breakfast, and go to work at whatever I had to do.

I spent some very happy days in this big house and made some friendships that have lasted up to the last few years, but I do not think that even one of my companions of those days, nearly fifty-four years ago, are still living; such is life. Death is no respecter of persons.

At the back of the "Big House" and facing the present Fort Garry gate stood the residence of the Hudson's Bay governor, but at that time, the lieutenant-governor of Manitoba, the Honourable A.G. Archibald resided there. It was a comfortable house, well-kept and shaded by fine trees, and had a fine garden in which the usual vegetables and small fruits were grown. I had the honour of being introduced to Mr. Archibald and his charming daughter and visited Government House once or twice during my stay at Fort Garry.

On each side of the square were warehouses in which were stored the thousands of bales of buffalo robes and furs until ready for shipment. In these were stored also thousands of dollars worth of merchandise of all kinds used in the fur trade.

In going through these stores you could get a very good idea of the resources of the country at that time: thousands of pelts of the different fur-bearing animals — beaver, bear, badger, otter, mink, wolf, wolverine, foxes of all kinds from the beautiful silver and black, down to the little prairie "red fox," and white polar bears from Hudson Bay. Also white arctic foxes from the same region, hundreds of moose and deer skins already tanned and smoked, ready to be made into leather coats and other garments that keep out the cold, as well as into moccasins. There were also many bales of buffalo and moose sinews that were used instead of thread for sewing the leather garments.

You could see also bales of something you had never heard of before; this was what is called "babiche" [bibiche]. It is made of the hide of buffalo, moose, or deer after the hair is scraped from the hide. The hide is cut into long lines or strings according to what use it is going to be put to. The finely cut "babiche" was used for netting snowshoes and the coarser stuff for repairing flat sleds used in winter, and also in repairing parts of the Red River carts when on a journey when time was a factor. I have seen a few of these old-time carts, the wheels of which looked as if they had been made mostly of "babiche" and buffalo bones. Still they were fit to travel and carry a load.

It would be almost impossible to produce a detailed list of the different things stored in those warehouses, so I must be content to say that all the needs of a man who was not too difficult to please could be supplied at short notice at any time, day or night.

Here also, stored for safety, was one of the large "Inland Canoes," the same as was used by Sir George Simpson every year [from Montreal to

Fort Garry] during his reign as governor of the Company. The canoe was about thirty feet long and had a five-foot beam, perhaps a little more. The crew consisted of eight or ten men, mostly Iroquois from Lachine near Montreal, and they were picked men, the best that could be obtained. It is said they used to make the trip from Montreal to Fort William in less than half the time spent by others making the trip. Sir George, they say, used to keep his men up to the mark by the judicious use of a little HBC rum, and, when the pace slackened, he would put his hand in the water and if the water did not run up his hand, he would say "hep! hep! hep!" and urge the men to renewed efforts.

There are many stories regarding Sir George Simpson that have been handed down from generation to generation by men connected with the Hudson's Bay Company. Some of the stories are to his credit, and some are otherwise. "*Requiescet in pace.*"

I now come to what interested me more than anything else at Fort Garry and that was the "Trading Shop" where all the business with the Indians and others was transacted. This shop stood at the southeast corner of the Fort, not far from where the [Winnipeg Electric Railway] car barns now stand. It was a two-storey building, built of logs, and boarded on the outside to make it look like a frame building. I was always pleased to be sent there, where I was supposed to get an insight into dealing with the Natives and Plains hunters who came to trade.

Here on the shelves were displayed everything that was needed for the Indian trade — red, white, blue, and green "HB" blankets, shrouds of all colours used for leggings by men and women alike, printed cotton of all the colours of the rainbow, blanket capotes of two or three different colours. Also found were fine cloth capotes with large brass buttons, flannel shirts of many colours, tartan shawls, and gala plaid tartan dress goods that would create envy in the heart of a Highlander or his wife. Some of these dress goods could not be bettered today for quality, and the prices were not high, when one thinks of the route over which these goods were brought — French merino of all shades, merino shawls of all shades and sizes, and a multitude of other lines of dress goods and men's furnishings.

The French Métis women showed a distinct preference for dark shades of dress goods. Nearly every one of them were dressed in black merino, with a black merino shawl thrown over their head "in lieu" of other head covering. The Native women, on the other hand, used their hard-earned buffalo robes and furs to deck themselves out in dresses and shawls of the most vibrant colours.

I was as much interested in the way in which trade was carried on with the Natives. An Indian would bring in his pack of furs or robes, place them on the counter, where they were sorted out by the trader and a valuation made by him. He would then hand the Indian the value of his stuff in "tokens," which were either round or square pieces of brass with the value stamped on each piece. These "tokens" ran in value from the standard of "One Made Beaver" down to a quarter of the same. [One Made Beaver was a unit of value equal to a prime adult beaver pelt. All other furs and trade items were measured against it.]

An Indian's idea of a fair trade means that he gets at least something for nothing. He always had his mind made up regarding what he wanted before coming to the store, and if he had a good supply of furs to trade he was easy to get along with, and soon completed his trading. On the other hand, the one who had made a poor hunt wants everything he sees and is hard to deal with, and he always ends up by asking for credit, which he generally gets, and seldom pays without regret. He is not naturally dishonest, but is "up against it," as we say, and puts off paying his debt as long as possible.

Hundreds of steel traps of different sizes hung on nails from the ceiling and dozens of guns of all sorts, from the cheapest "flintlock" to the double-barrelled, fine precision cap article, stood in racks along the wall.

There was nothing that a Native could possibly want that could not be found in that store. A great many small articles were given *gratis* to an Indian after he finished trading, items such as awls, flints for his gun, "gun-worms" with which to clean his gun, a steel that he used along with a flint to make a fire or light his pipe. These two articles were used along with "touch-wood" or charred rags, and some whom I have known, could start a fire nearly as quickly as with matches. Other articles such as thimbles, fish hooks, and a dozen or two brass tacks were given to any older Native woman who happened to be along with the man who was trading. No Indian ever left the shop after he was done trading without a "gratuity" of tea, sugar, and tobacco.

In the middle of the Fort's square stood a tall flagstaff from which, during daylight, waved the HBC ensign. A bell woke us up in the morning, called us to dinner, and told us when our work for the day was over.

The officers' mess in those days at Fort Garry was a good place to be at mealtime. There was a first-class cook in charge of the kitchen, and two or three waiters attended to our wants when at table. Breakfast and lunch were completed as one pleased, but dinner, which was at seven o'clock in the evening, was regimental to a degree. All the officers of the Company at the fort, whether married or single, were supposed to attend, and though dress clothes were not insisted on, we were supposed to attend in our best clothes. Each clerk, according to rank, had his fixed place at the table, the juniors sitting "below the salt" as the saying is. One of the highest officers sat at the head of the table and another at the foot. "Grace" was said by the officer in charge, before and after the meal. We had wine on the table at our Sunday dinner, but none on weekdays.

I visited the bastion where Thomas Scott[6] was placed before his execution by orders of Louis Riel, but found nothing to interest me.

This year, 1872, was one of the grasshopper years in Manitoba and up to that time I had no idea that there could be so many grasshoppers in the world, and I began to think that poor old Pharaoh did not have an easy time when he undertook to keep the Children of Israel making bricks without straw in Egypt. The grasshoppers arrived in the night and before daylight you could hear the sound of their wings as they were driven before the wind. In the morning the sky was grey and clouded with the pests. One could not see the sun plainly. It was a veritable blizzard of grasshoppers. They landed anywhere and everywhere. If a door was left open for a few minutes, hundreds of hoppers filled the room and it was impossible to walk anywhere outside without killing thousands and getting your footwear in the dirty mess.

On the day of the arrival of the grasshoppers I was in the office, not very busy, when I was sent for by Mr. McTavish. He told me that the Hudson's Bay Company chief commissioner, the Honourable Donald A. Smith (afterwards Lord Strathcona) was going out to his place at "Silver Heights" and wanted someone to drive him, and thought I would do. I went over to the stable where the horses were ready for me and then to the commissioner's office for Mr. Smith, and we started off on our drive. We drove through masses of grasshoppers and had not gone far before the smashed insects were running down the tires like thick soup.

We went out to St. James where binders and mowers had been going all night in an effort to save some of the grain crops. The commissioner visited the farm of Robert Tait and found all hands hard at work, cutting down the half-ripened crops of oats and wheat. On the farm at Silver Heights things were no better than elsewhere, and, after giving orders to the foreman, we turned homeward. The swarms of grasshoppers got thicker at noon and the sun could only be seen very dimly. We went home by another route and drove through Fort Osborne barracks where many of the soldiers were living in tents. Here we saw parties of soldiers sweeping up the hoppers and shovelling them into wheelbarrows that they emptied into the Assiniboine River to float away. The grasshoppers continued for, I think, two or three weeks.

A few days later Mr. McTavish sent for me to come to his office where he gave me orders to get ready to proceed to Norway House at the north end of Lake Winnipeg. I wanted to go West to the prairies, but more than anything, I wished to get away to be amongst the Indians. I was delighted at the news and after leaving the office I think I turned handsprings all the way to my quarters. I must have acted a little wild because one of the clerks who happened to be in the house asked me if I had a "bee in my bonnet."

I had no idea of when I was to leave for Norway House, and, as I had to get an "outfit" of clothing and other things better suited for the more northern climate, I went back to the office and asked Mr. McTavish when he thought the boats from Norway House would arrive. He said he could not be sure, but I would have two or three weeks anyway before the boats were here. So that night I wrote a long letter to my father, telling him where I was being sent to and asking for money to get properly fitted out. I also told him one or two of the exaggerated stories that were told to me on my first night in Fort Garry. I warned him that if he did not wish to hear of his eldest son slowly starving to death or being killed by blood-thirsty Natives or devoured by wild animals, he should at once send me a good gun to enable me to hunt for my living and also be able to protect myself from wild animals and wilder Indians. My letter had the desired effect on my dear father. A good-sized cheque came to hand in about ten days and a very nice double-barrelled gun came to me by express the day before I left Norway House. [Mail service would have gone by boat down the Red River to Grand Forks, North Dakota, and east by rail to London, Ontario, and returned by that route.]

Very little office work was given to me after I had received my orders for Norway House and so I spent most of my time in the trading store, I learned quite a few Indian words, such as the names of the more requested articles of trade, and I was very pleased when a Native asked for an axe, knife, powder, and shot, and I could understand him and give him what he wanted without an interpreter.

I often visited my friend Walt Hyman and on one of these visits I was introduced to one of Manitoba's biggest men. This was the Honourable James McKay, but he was mostly spoken of as "Jim." He was the largest man I ever saw, outside of a freak show. At that time he weighed around four-hundred pounds. He had a buckboard that was made especially for his use and that of his wife, who was nearly as big as he was. I mentioned that I was related to Chief Factor B.R. Ross, and, as the Honourable "Jim" and he were close friends, I was well received and invited to call on him at his fine residence, which was called Deer Lodge and is still one of the show places around Winnipeg.

Jim McKay was a great friend of the Sioux, not only on this side of the line, but also in the United States, and it was said that when the Sioux across the border in the States could not obtain ammunition, they came to Manitoba and were well-supplied by "Jim" as they called him. He, however, could not safely cross the line into the States. I did hear that the American authorities more than once tried to get him, but never succeeded in doing so. They blamed "Jim" to some extent for supplying the Sioux with ammunition shortly before the "Minnesota Massacre"[7] in 1862. What truth there is in this, if any, I do not know.

I visited him at Deer Lodge and spent some pleasant hours with him and his wife and daughter Mary. He had a fine collection of Indian stone pipes of many colours and shapes, bows and arrows, beaded and feathered "tea bags" and tobacco pouches worked in beads and porcupine quills, stone axes, spears and spear heads made of stone and copper, headdresses of many coloured feathers, belts worked in coloured beads and dyed porcupine quills, earthen jars of many shapes and sizes made by the Sioux in the United States, saddles ornamented with beads, brass tacks and coloured porcupine quills, besides one or two scalps, which he showed me on the quiet. All the servants around his house and on his farm were Sioux Indians.

I took very little interest in what was called the City of Winnipeg. There are still in the city, however, a few names that appeared on the fronts of stores at that early date. J.H. Ashdown being the most prominent. Holy Trinity Church, in those days, stood near the corner of what is now Portage and Main streets and was under the charge of the Venerable Archdeacon McLean, afterwards Bishop of Saskatchewan. I know him very well, his having come from London, Ontario. My father and Archdeacon McLean were both connected with Huron College, which has since my time developed into Western University where my father was, at the time of his death in 1878, a Classics professor.

What is now Main Street, was in those days, a prairie road and a very wet and muddy one at that. I have seen dozens of wagons and carts "mired down" up to the hubs, between where now stands the Royal Alexander Hotel and the corner of Portage and Main streets. One of the worst mud holes on the road was to be found about where McLean and Garland have their store at present.

In those days a good-sized creek ran from a swamp or small lake rather, from where the General Hospital[8] now stands. This creek flowed through what is now Market Square and emptied into the Red River. There was a wooden bridge over this creek where the Union Bank Building now stands at the corner of Main Street and Williams Avenue. This bridge was always out of repair and there were accidents nearly every day. While I was at Fort Garry, a team of oxen and a wagon went through the guards on the side of the bridge and landed at the bottom in the mud and water. One of the animals had its leg broken and had to be killed.

Horse racing took place on Main Street every day, not excepting Sunday, and sometimes the betting ran high, some of the Métis losing all they had in the world, such as horses and carts, and in some cases, their tents and household goods. The French-speaking Métis was, and is, an inveterate gambler and a good loser.

The forks of the Red and Assiniboine rivers was a great fishing place in those days. All sorts of fish were to be found — sturgeon, catfish, goldeyes, white fish, pike (or Jack pike), suckers, etc. It was difficult to row across the river without touching a net and the fishermen did a good trade in the "City."

During my stay at Fort Garry a great Methodist divine came to the country on a tour of inspection. He gave a lecture one evening. This gentleman was the renowned William Morley Punshon.[9] He gave his lecture in a warehouse that belonged to the Hudson's Bay Company and that stood on the bank of the Assiniboine, about halfway between where the Car Barns now stand, and where it joins the Red River. The Honourable Donald A. Smith was chairman and the Hudson's Bay Company employees turned out "en masse" to attend the lecture. The reverend gentleman's text was: "And there were giants in the land in those days." He gave a short sketch of many of the most prominent men in Canada and the United States at that period, not forgetting our

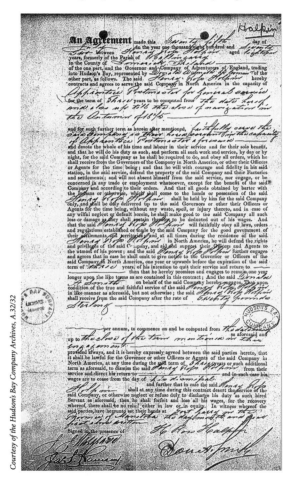

Courtesy of the Hudson's Bay Company Archives, A.32/32

Henry Ross Halpin's Hudson's Bay Company contract, 1872. Note the signature of Donald Smith, governor of the Hudson's Bay Company. He was later a founder of the Canadian Pacific Railway, and received the title Lord Strathcona.

esteemed Governor Honourable D.A. Smith. It was altogether an interesting discourse. A collection, which was a worthwhile one, was taken up. It was suggested by the Honourable Donald A. Smith who, as chairman, called for a vote of thanks to the reverend lecturer and referred to him as " a Prince among men, etc., etc." I guess Mr. Punshon thought that each one of the Company people had private fortunes. The collection, I heard, ran close to $500.00. Outside of Hudson's Bay Company employees there may have been twenty people at the lecture, but not more. Mr. Punshon was entertained at Government House during his stay in Winnipeg. All the Hudson's Bay Company employees from the governor down, turned out to see him off on the boat on his leaving for home.

At this time, though there was no news from Norway House, I did not find the days too long. On one or two occasions I had the pleasure of a ride on horseback to Lower Fort Garry or the "Stone Fort," as it was called in those days. On my trips I was the bearer of important letters for the officer in charge there. There was no mail service between the two places. I was circumspect on my way down with the letters, but on my way back, I had a race with every Métis rider on the trail. The horse given me for these trips was an old buffalo runner, so some of the men I raced with got quite a surprise when I left them far in the rear without trouble.

The boat from Norway House arrived towards the end of July and so I was all ready to go. I lost no time in packing up for the trip.

2 Lake Winnipeg, a York Boat, and an Ox

*T*he boat I was going to Norway House on did not belong to the Norway House outfit. It was one of six that had come from Oxford House [in northeast Manitoba] with the last winter's catch of fur and that were to take back supplies, part of which were for Norway House with the balance for Oxford.

We left Fort Garry early in the morning. A mist hung over the river. One could hardly see either bank from the middle of the stream and there was no sound except the noise made by the boatmen as they pulled on the long heavy oars, but as the sun rose higher all this was changed. The mist cleared away and we found ourselves floating down between green poplar-covered banks with here and there a farmhouse to be seen almost concealed by tall oak or elm trees. In one hour or so we passed down the St. Andrews Rapids. I thought they were big and swift, but I was to see rapids later on that made these appear as little more than a ripple on the water.

We got to the Stone Fort [also known as Lower Fort Garry, north of Winnipeg] at noon, and had dinner there, and after our meal I received a very unpleasant surprise. I learned that four oxen were being sent out in the boats, two for Oxford and two for Norway House. I could not understand at first how they were going to get the animals into the boats, how they were going to lie down, etc., but these animals had been trained just for an occasion like this, and, when brought down to where

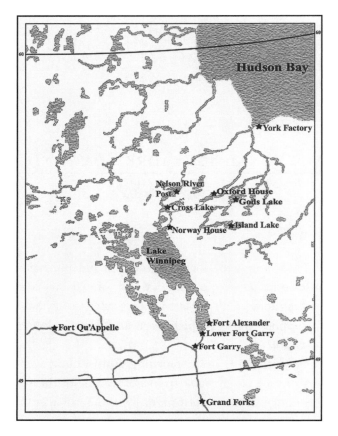

Trading Posts Associated with Halpin's Early Career in the Fur Trade.

the boats were tied to the dock, each one stepped into the stern section of the boat assigned to it [one per boat] without the slightest hesitation. A pen about five feet wide had been made at the stern of each boat and strong boards were nailed together behind the animal to prevent it from backing overboard. The boards in front were fastened with strong ropes that could be quickly untied in case of accident and allowed the ox to be taken ashore to graze when we stopped for meals or at night where we camped.

I did not mind, having friend ox for a companion. He acted like a gentleman while in the calm water in the river, but when we reached the lake where it is always more or less rough, things began to happen. Mr.

Ox tried to lie down but could not manage to do so. He then tried to get a drink out of the lake and had it not been that the boards in front of him were strong, he would have gone headfirst overboard. When he found that it was not easy to move, he became quiet and I felt rather sorry for him. I got hold of an empty bucket that was in the boat and gave him a good drink.

About sundown we reached Willow Point, about ten miles from the mouth of the Red River and at least sixty miles from Fort Garry, which we had left in the morning. This was my first night in camp in Manitoba. When the boats were tied up, the oxen were taken ashore. There was a quantity of fine green willows and reeds, but no grass. The infernal grasshoppers had been ahead of us and devoured everything in the way of grass. However, the oxen seemed to enjoy the reeds and willows, so what did it matter?

The man allotted to me for my servant[1] during the voyage soon got my tent up, brought my bedding from the boat, and prepared my supper, which I soon finished, and had the rest of the evening to think things over. Each of the crews of the four boats had its own campfire and cooking outfit, and all were soon busy eating. Their rations were mostly pemmican and flour made into a sort of thick soup. These articles are quite palatable.

Pemmican, which was just boiled and the water then poured off, and to which a little flour is added, was placed in a frying pan until well-browned and crisp, is called "Resheau" and tasted a good deal like bologna sausage. I never got to like it; it was too rich and always gave me what is called heartburn.

Soon after supper the boatmen started to gamble. The game played was something like what we call "hide the slipper" and could be played by as many as wanted to. At the same time, the game was played with a drum accompaniment. I watched the pastime for a while and then retired to my tent to sleep if possible, but which I felt would be difficult owing to the music outside my tent.

I was not long in my tent before the flap was thrown open and a head of what I took to be a large crane was poked inside. It gave me several hard pecks with its beak. I knew there was some fun afoot because I could hear the men laughing outside. So I rose up and went outside with the crane following after me. Mr. Crane drove me out to the fire, pecking at me now and then. The "crane" spoke in Indian, so I had to get one of the men to tell me what he wanted. What he wanted was a treat of tobacco for the crew of the boat I was a passenger on. I did not have sufficient with me to treat the crowd, so I promised that on our arrival at Norway House the tobacco would be forthcoming. This was satisfactory and I was allowed to return to my tent to try to sleep. (After we arrived at Norway House I gave each man a good supply of tobacco and I was told by Mr. Ross that this performance was gone through with every young clerk that crossed Lake Winnipeg for the first time.)

I was called out of my sleep before daylight next morning and found everything ready to start. The oxen were already in the boats. So after a hasty cup of tea and a biscuit, I embarked and off we started, the men on the oars as it was quite calm on the lake. However, it did not remain so very long. We had gone only a few miles from our camp when a light south wind sprang up. It was strong enough for us to get up sail, for which the boatmen were not sorry.

In three or four hours, tea was made on board the boat. A piece of flat rock and a large worn-out kettle, in which the fire was made,

Courtesy of the Glenbow Archives, NA–1847–5

A York boat under sail.

were used to boil our water to make the tea. I enjoyed my breakfast, but should not have done so, had I known what was ahead of us during the rest of the day.

That morning I noticed quite a number of grasshoppers floating in the water but did not give them a second thought. I was reading a book that I had taken along when the steersman touched me on the shoulder and told me to look ahead. This I did and was astonished at the queer colour of the water. In a few minutes we knew the cause. The boat was sailing through grasshoppers floating on the water, six inches deep and reaching right and left further than we could see. The smell was disgusting. We sailed on for four or five hours before we were out of the grasshopper mess. In that time we must have travelled thirty or forty miles. To use a slang expression, "some grasshoppers, eh what!"

But there was worse ahead of us than the grasshoppers. We had not left them far behind when it began to blow a little too hard for the comfort of our bovine passenger. The ox became restless, and, at times when a wave splashed into the boat, it would try to avoid the water, which made matters worse. Had we been near land we would have gone ashore, but we were several miles out in the lake, so there was nothing to do but to push on. The wind increased and of course the waves grew larger and quite a lot of water came over the gunwales of the boat. Poor Mr. Ox groaned, either with fear or seasickness, but whatever it was that made him groan, it kept him still for awhile.

The wind increased to such an extent that we had to take a double reef in our sail, which of course hindered our speed. The boat was now about three miles from "Bull Head," which we were trying to reach, where we could go ashore and wait until the wind moderated. The wind blew harder than ever and a thunder and lightning storm came up with a heavy downpour of rain that added to our troubles. When about a half a mile from Bull Head, the guide in the boat I was in signalled to the other boats that he was going to land. So the other three boats drew in towards us and it was well they did. A very fierce gust of wind came and our mast snapped off, almost in the middle. Our big sail went overboard and we were pitched about like a cork between the high waves. I thought any moment our vessel was going to capsize, and I prepared for a swim. I removed my boots and coat and was ready to jump at a moment's notice. We were now drifting with the wind, our boat broadside to the waves that broke over us every minute, but soon, two of the other boats drew alongside of us and ropes were thrown, which were tied to the iron ring in the bow of ours. One of the two now moved ahead of us and our boat was soon positioned before the wind. We reached shore in a little cove below Bull Head, and our troubles were over for a while anyway.

Our boat was nearly a third full of water and many of the bales of merchandise soaked through. We opened a number in order to dry them if possible. Most of the wet bales contained blankets, which can stand a lot of wetting without being damaged to any great extent. Some bales of printed cottons were very wet and when dried presented quite a different pattern from that intended by the manufacturer. Our ox did not suffer much and was quite ready to eat when taken ashore.

We camped at Bull Head for the night and tried our best to dry what we could of the wettest bales. The pasture for our oxen was good at this point and they were full when taken to the boats in the morning. The grasshoppers failed to alight here. I guess a change of wind forced them down into the lake, which was a blessing. (When I arrived at Norway House I was told that only a few had appeared there and no harm was done to the garden.)

We left Bull Head early in the morning with a fair wind. A new mast had been placed in our boat and things were shipshape once more. We sailed along all day with only one stop of about an hour to give the oxen a chance to stretch their legs and get a little to eat.

We camped at Rabbit Point, a lovely spot on the east shore of the lake. There was fine grazing ground for our poor oxen and they certainly made use of their time ashore. (There is a beautiful sandy beach at Rabbit Point and some day some far-seeing man will discover it, get busy, and before long there will be one of the finest summer resorts on Lake Winnipeg established.) [...][2]

Fine weather and fair wind continued next day. We made good progress and camped for the night at Kettle Islands where the Hudson's Bay Company had a man to look after their two hundred train [sled] dogs during the summer months. I did not enjoy camping on this island.

I could not stand the smell of the fish nor the dogs either. So before dark I got my man to take my bedding to the boat and I slept there, but the dogs kept me awake trying to get into the boat. I was not sorry when we left the place early the next morning.

I guess the weatherman was trying to make up to us for the trouble he gave us on our first day on the lake. There was a fair wind and the guide said if it kept up we might reach our destination tomorrow night, and anyway he was sure he would get there early the next day if nothing happened to keep us back. But something did happen. The wind went round to the north and we had to land on one of the Spider Islands [on the northeast side of Lake Winnipeg] before noon and we had to stay there for a day and a half. With the change of the wind there came rain and I had to stay inside my tent all day.

In the evening the rain stopped, and, as the night was warm, I had my first taste of Lake Winnipeg mosquitoes. I had never used a mosquito bar [an insect repellent bar that would be rubbed on the skin] at home. No one at Fort Garry had mentioned the need of one. I had to suffer all night. I tried to make the tent mosquito proof, but did not succeed. I never travelled in summer again without a mosquito bar.

It was here I first came in contact with the Lake Winnipeg Natives. Two or three families were camped on the island and were busy drying and smoking whitefish. I found these people to be rather dirty in their habits but they were, notwithstanding, a simple, good-natured lot of people. There were lots of children in the camp and it was here I got my first lesson as to the proper way to eat and enjoy a fish diet.

I was sitting outside my tent in the morning, and, hearing a child crying as if it had been hurt in some way, I walked towards the tent near which the baby was sitting quite naked on the bare rock. The crying child was a boy, I should say about a year-and-a-half old, and he did not seem to have much the matter with him. I made up my mind at once that his lungs were all right. His mother was working close to him, but paid no attention to the cries he gave at short intervals. He began to cry louder than ever, so at last his mother thought he might want a plaything of some kind. So she gave him the first thing that was handy, which to my horror, was a sharp butcher knife. The baby played with the knife for a few minutes and then started to cry once more. Then it struck his mother that he might be hungry so she went to a large kettle that stood nearby and took out a big piece of boiled fish, put it in a pan, and gave it to the baby. This will be a case of cold-blooded murder, I thought, for I was sure the baby would choke on the bones. I watched the baby for some time, ready to give assistance if it was needed, but nothing happened. That baby would take a handful of fish and stuff it into his little mouth, chew for a minute or so, and the fish bones came out at the corner of his mouth and fell on his little bare legs. He did not seem to know that fish had bones. He reminded me of the machine used to take the seeds out of raisins.

We left Spider Islands in the afternoon. There was no wind so the men had to make use of their oars. This was one of the "Red Letter" days in my life for the reason that I killed my first bear. It was not, however, a fair test of my quality as a hunter because we came across the poor bear in the water. He was swimming from one of the small rocky islands to the mainland. One shot from my new gun finished him and the men pulled him into the boat. The bear was very fat. I did not enjoy the meat, which was on the "menu" for supper. It had a very fishy taste, the bear having lived principally on fish all summer. One of the men got the hide, which was of very little value. I had the claws cut off and later sent them to my sister in London, Ontario.

We camped that night at what is now called "Warren Landing." Mosquitoes were there in millions and "smudges" had to be made to drive them off. The smoke, I thought, was almost as bad as the mosquitoes. I had my supper in my tent. It was next to impossible to eat outside because every time you opened your mouth, mosquitoes would get in along with your food.

The Hudson's Bay Company carried on a sturgeon fishery at this point. I had eaten sturgeon but had never seen one alive until now, and I was surprised at their size. Some I saw here weighed over two-hundred pounds and I was told that many of the fish caught weighed even more than that. These sturgeons were very carefully taken out of the net so as not to injure them in any way. They were then placed in a "tank boat" used for that purpose, the water being changed every day. Every day or so this boat made a trip to Norway House, twenty or more miles away. The fish were then removed from the tank and placed in pens made for that purpose and taken from there as needed.

(The man in charge of the sturgeon fishery at that time was Hector Morrison, one of the oldest employees at Norway House. He had been in the service for over fifty years. He looked to me like one of the old Highlanders you see in pictures. After the fishing was over and he returned to his home at Norway House, I got to know and respect the old man. When the long dreary winter came, many times it was two or three o'clock in morning before I could leave him after listening to his very interesting stories of the old times far back when he came to the country. Many of the tales he told me were on a par with "Alice in Wonderland" or "Jack and the Bean Stalk," but they were none the worse for that. He believed most of these Indian tales, having been so long in the country. He was more than half-Indian.

Hector had a large family, mostly girls. They all married pretty well, one of them being the wife of the late Roderick Smith of Selkirk. A granddaughter is chief clerk in the Selkirk Post Office. Hector Morrison died only a few years ago when over ninety years of age.)

The next day our boats reached Norway House about noon.[3] I was glad to be at the end of my journey. Chief Factor Roderick Ross was a brother-in-law of my relative Chief Factor B.R. Ross, so I received a warm welcome. D.C. McTavish, a brother of the officer in charge of Fort Garry, J.H. McTavish [chief factor] was second in command at Norway House.

Mr. Ross took me to his house and introduced me to his wife and family, who all, owing to my connection with the family, treated me like one of his sons, and I found myself at home, for how long, of course, I did not know.

3   Norway House

*I*t was at Norway House, the day after my arrival, that I first witnessed a prize fight for a belt, which was a fine piece of Indian work and represented the championship of the North Country. This belt had been fought for, for many years, and besides the belt and the championship, the Hudson's Bay Company gave a prize to the winner of the fight. Some years the fight took place at York Factory, but it could take place at any of the large HBC posts where the champion happened to be living and if anyone could be found to accept his challenge. The prize given by the Company was generally a suit of clothes and a tall old-fashioned beaver hat, trimmed with red feathers.

The men, who were going to fight this time, were both French Half-breeds. One came along as a steersman in one of the boats belonging to the Athabasca brigade, which consisted of about fifteen "York" boats. The crews numbered in the neighbourhood of one hundred and twenty. The brigade from "Île-à-la-Crosse" was also in camp there on their way to York Factory. There must have been altogether fifty or sixty "York" boats tied up along the riverbank. This meant at least three hundred and fifty men comprised the crews. The champion of last year, who was now ready to defend his title, was also a steersman in the "Île-à-la-Crosse" brigade.

The fight came off late in the afternoon. There were no preliminaries, no handshaking, no time lost in talking, as all present had for years known the rules or rather the "no rules" of the game. Bare fists were used and nothing was barred in the fighting with the exceptions of "eye-gouging" and biting.

A sort of war whoop was now heard in the champion's camp pitched near the Swan River rock, a high rocky point a little up river from the fort. Soon after Pierre Gendrie, the champion, with his escort, came into view. He was a big man, at least six feet tall, and would weigh close to two hundred pounds. He was dressed in his trousers; he wore heavy boots, a wonderful tall hat with red cock feathers, and his championship belt. He came along, calling at the top of his voice for anyone to come out and win the belt if he could. Of course, the parties to the fight were already known, and as soon as the champion had reached the middle of the camp, the challenger, a man named Gregoire who belonged to the Saskatchewan brigade from Edmonton, stepped out from his tent, and asked what all the noise was about. A few words were exchanged by the fighters, and then the fight was on. It was a fight to the finish and both men were out for blood.

The challenger started the fight by jumping about five feet up in the air, kicking Gendrie on the breast, but did not knock him down. It was now Gendrie's turn; he rushed at Gregoire, managed to get on his back, and kicked and pounded him wherever he could. In a minute or two Gendrie had Gregoire on the ground.

Gregoire, at last, managed to stand up but with Gendrie still hanging on to him. They wrestled for a couple of minutes, then, to my great astonishment, Gregoire managed to get Gendrie on his back on the ground, and sat on his breast and pounded his face for several minutes, Gendrie all the time struggling to get to his feet, which after awhile he managed to do. By this time both men were covered with blood from head to foot, but the champion looked to me as if he was getting the worst of the deal. Some of their friends went to the river for water and dashed it over both men, and in less than a few minutes, the fight resumed.

I never had seen a real fight before; all fighting at school had been with our fists and fairplay was the order of the day, and no one was ever hurt much beyond a black eye or so, but let me get back to the fight. Gregoire, so far as I could judge, was having the best of it. He was a much lighter man than Gendrie and about the same height. About this time Gendrie threw Gregoire to the ground and gave him a couple of hard kicks before he could get up. Upon rising he flew at Gendrie, got him by the hair, and pounded away at his face and the side of his head. Blood was now running from the mouths and noses of both men, but though their features were quite unrecognizable the fight went on, both men showing no sign of giving up.

The fight had now lasted for nearly half an hour. Both men became more wary. They came to a clinch, now and then, for a rest, it seemed to me. About this time there were several good exhibitions of footwork. Both men would jump in the air and kick out at each other. They looked like two big roosters. Once more Gregoire managed to get on Gendrie's back, and after a couple of minutes threw him to the ground where he lay a few seconds. In those few seconds, Gregoire kicked him fiercely in the ribs and stomach.

Gendrie had three ribs broken and was pretty badly hurt otherwise. Gregoire was now champion; he went over to where Gendrie lay on the ground, took off the champion's belt, held it up in the air, and challenged one and all to dispute his right to it. As none appeared to be anxious to take up the dare, Gregoire soon left for his camp, surrounded by his friends and admirers, who kept shouting his praises until they reached his camp. I found out the next day that Gregoire also had a broken rib and was nearly giving up when his chance came to put Gendrie out of business. Poor Gendrie remained at Norway House for a month before he was fit to travel and went back to his post by one of the last boats in the fall.

I have seen many of these fights of which I shall speak later. Gregoire held the belt for two years but, in an encounter at York Factory, lost the belt in a fight with an Iroquois from Trois Rivières, near Montreal. The Iroquois lost it in a few days to a man from Fort Qu'Appelle, named La Roche, who later became a great fighter and held the championship for several years. Later on, I shall tell you of the rise and fall of La Roche.

I shall now try to give you some idea of how Norway House, and its people, impressed me. The Hudson's Bay Company establishment, Norway House, is built on an island. It is bounded on one side by Jack

Courtesy of the Glenbow Archives, NB-40-14

An interior view of Norway House, Hudson's Bay Company, taken in 1932.

River, which flows out of Playgreen Lake, and on the other, by what was at that time spoken of as Little Lea River, which emptied into Little Playgreen Lake at Norway House. The buildings were situated at the furthest northeast point of Jack Island. Norway House is called *He-noo-say-sei-pee Was-Ka gon*, which means, in English "Jack fish house."

In my time the buildings were surrounded by a high fence, made of strong poles that stood upright in the ground to a height of ten or twelve feet. In the front of the fort, facing the river, was a high archway fitted with strong doors that were closed every night in summer at nine o'clock, and not opened again until the next morning at seven o'clock. On one side of these large doors there was a small door that could be used when needed, but though there was no special reason given, those living in the fort were supposed to be there by nine o'clock. This door had a padlock that was locked at nine o'clock. There was a hole in the door through which the padlock could be reached by hand, and each officer or clerk had a key that fitted the padlock. I don't think these keys were much used because there was nothing to interest one outside after dark.

Norway House was, for many years, the meeting place for the Council of the Northern Departments. Here were discussed plans for the future endeavours of the vast business of the great Company. Chief factors from every district arrived at a set time and met with the governor or the chief commissioner with whom they talked over the most important items in connection with the districts where they were in charge. Here were made changes, from year to year, of the officers attached to certain districts. The Council lasted for about a month. It was a busy and heartbreaking month for the clerks of the establishment and all were glad when it came to an end and the commissioner and factors left for their own homes.

The interior of the fort at Norway House was like most of the other District Headquarters that I have seen. The "Big House," which contained the offices and council chamber, faced towards the river. It was a large two-storey log building with a facing of ship-lap [clapboard siding]. The upper storey was laid out in a number of rooms that were occupied by the factors attending the council, when in session, and were used also by any visitors who happened along. The officers' mess was in the lower part of the house next to the office, and one of the lower rooms, also on the ground floor, was used as a library and contained a fine lot of various kinds of reading matter amongst which were some very valuable old books.

One side of the square was taken up by three long warehouses. These at times were filled with supplies from York Factory, which were sent up in the late summer so as to be ready the following summer for shipment in the boats that came from the Athabasca and McKenzie River districts as the trip to York Factory was found to be too long. This enabled the boats to return to their far northern posts before there was a chance of their being frozen in and not reaching their destinations.

On the opposite side of the square there was a long row of buildings — trading shop, provision store, store for employees, and warehouse for the Norway House District only. There were four houses fitted up and furnished for use of Hudson's Bay Company officers travelling from one district to another in summer, and for those who were delayed by the non-arrival of the boats in which they were to proceed on their journey to wherever they were going. There was also a long narrow building in which fishing nets were made or repaired ready for the fall fishing. Fifty thousand whitefish were used every winter as food for the employees and sled dogs.

There were thirty-five or forty employees engaged under contract for a three-to-five-year period, and perhaps as many more temporary servants employed during the winter as wood cutters, dog drivers, etc.

There was a fine large garden in my time at Norway House, and it had a very interesting history, which is as follows: About fifty years before my arrival at this post, a certain factor, Donald Ross by name, came to take charge of this post. He may have been a vegetarian. Anyway, upon his arrival at the post, no garden was to be seen. He was determined to have one and when the old-time Hudson's Bay Company men wanted anything, they got it, if it was possible to get. There were places on the mainland where a good garden could be had without much trouble, but to move all the buildings to the garden site was not to be thought of, so Factor Ross made up his mind to move a garden or the makings of one to a place near the fort. Therefore, in the spring after his arrival, he picked out the place where the garden should be set out, and he had a hundred men and women and ten York boats or more move soil from across the lake, carry it in bags up the bank from where the boats landed, and empty the bags on the garden site. I was told it took about five month's hard work before one could notice where the hundreds of tons of soil had been dumped. At any rate, Mr. Factor Ross had a small garden the summer after his arrival, and during his stay of many years I believe he added a little each year until the garden reached its present dimensions.

Inside the garden, the day after I arrived, I was much surprised at what I saw — red, white, and black currents, fully ripe, and what surprised me much more was the fine crop of cucumbers and tomatoes. The tomatoes did not ripen on the vines, but did ripen after being taken into the house. All other common garden vegetables were represented and a good crop was harvested in the fall.

The only trouble the garden gave was with regard to the drainage. The soil was not deep and where the snowfall was heavy, or it rained much in the spring, the water used to lodge in the rock basin underneath the soil. There was no outlet to drain away the water, so the garden had to be pumped out at certain intervals. A large barrel with the bottom removed, specifically made for the purpose, had been sunk to bedrock, and when the water rose to a certain height in the barrel, pumping was resorted to.

There was, in my time, a sun dial in the middle of the garden that had been placed there by Sir John Franklin[1] a few years before he left on his tragic journey in search of the Northwest Passage.

At the back of the fort outside the stockade were the workshops in which different trades were carried on — boat building, blacksmith's work, carpenter's shop, harness shop, and last, but not least, a large bakery for providing the whole establishment with bread. The engaged permanent servants had a large building to themselves. It contained twenty-five or thirty bedrooms and a large room used as a mess and recreation room. The very best the country could supply in the way of food was provided for all employees in the service. The married employees had each a house for themselves.

There was at that time no resident minister at the fort but a religious service was held every Sunday in the officers' mess room in the "Big House." The Reverend E.R. Young[2] from the Rossville Methodist Mission, about three miles across the lake from the fort, looked after our spiritual welfare. He was a very fine man, a good preacher, and more than all, in the eyes of the Indian population, he was a good man in a boat in the summer and was hard to beat in winter, either on snowshoes or driving dogs when he went to visit some of his flock many days' journey away in the bush. (He was, I believe, a nephew of Egerton Ryerson, one of Morley Punshon's "giants"[3] who was much interested in education in the middle part of the last century. Young died in England many years ago. He wrote several stories for boys, which were published in England.)

Across the river from the fort was the cemetery that contained, chiselled on the headstones, the names of families connected with the Hudson's Bay Company for a hundred years or more. Some of the stones were in bad repair. This is a grave subject and I shall not continue it further.

I had nothing much to do for two or three weeks after I arrived at Norway House, as Mr. Ross said, to give me a chance to "find my feet." I spent a lot of time in the trading shop and a lot more time paddling all over the lake in a canoe with any young Indian I could persuade to go with me. I soon got used to canoeing, and inside of a month I could go anywhere by myself, but I liked to have someone with me, and, if possible, I never took anyone that could speak English. By the fall I had a couple of hundred Indian words fixed in my memory. I never spoke English to an Indian if I could help it and I may say here that at the end of two years I could speak "Swampy" Cree like a Native.

About the middle of September of that year, 1872, I had my first sight of the Nelson River. I went away with a party of ten men to a place where there was good timber and our purpose was to procure certain kinds of trees. The large roots of these, when sawn up, were used for "sterns" and "ribs" of the "York" boats that were to be built during the winter.

I had a splendid time. I hunted every day and managed to keep the camp supplied with ducks. On the river and in the swamps there were ducks by the hundreds and the woods were full of partridges.

On one occasion I shot at, but missed a moose. I am afraid the moose scared me. I was sitting on the riverbank near where my canoe was tied, when suddenly I heard a noise behind me and when I turned around to see what caused it, the moose was only ten yards away on his way to the river. I grabbed my gun and let fly at him with no result that I could see and when I fired the second barrel at him, he was too far away for me to do him any harm. After this, I always kept one barrel of my gun loaded with either buckshot or ball. That same afternoon I shot my first beaver and found the meat to be as good as I was told it was.

It was about three weeks before we returned to the fort. I remember we had a nice little snowstorm on our way back home. I do not think I shall ever forget those three weeks spent in the bush. It was the first real holiday in my life. I was only a boy, carefree and happy. and in the surroundings I always wished for. I think I was nearer to God and the heart of things than ever I was before. I was and am still fond of company, but at that time when I got away from the camp, up along the long stretches of the river with no sound that in anyway resembled the everyday turmoil of civilization, I felt quite sure I did not wish a companion and was glad to be alone to watch nature in all of its pristine glory.

The scenery was simply grand. All the colours of the rainbow were seen in the ever-changing lights and shadows that fell on the waters of the swift flowing river or on the forest trees. The leaves of summer were now changing from green to the most exquisite colours. The water in the river was smooth and unbroken by any wind and glided on its way to the sea. The heavens were clear, not a cloud to be seen. Dozens of islands, large and small of every shape, looked as if at sometime or other they were thrown from the sky to fall where they might. I used to lie on my back and look up to where we have been taught to believe Heaven is, and would wonder if it could possibly be more beautiful, more satisfying than where I was. At that time I could not make up my mind.

During the fall and well on into the winter I was employed in the trading shop and I am glad to say I made good progress in my knowledge of the language and in the mode of dealing with our principal customers, the Indians. After it froze up I tried my hand at trapping, but the results were small. I had much better luck going after the partridges and rabbits. I paid an old woman with some tea and sugar to come out to the bush and teach me how to set snares. I soon became quite expert at this business and generally got eight or ten rabbits from my snares each day. After the snow came, I made several trips into the bush, along with the men, to bring back the deer and moose meat killed by our hunters for use at the fort.

I came along very well and soon learned to drive dogs, just as well as my companions, but I wanted a dog team of my own, but how to get them, I did not know. I did not like to ask my father for any more money just then. A good team of dogs with harness and "carriole" [sled] cost in the neighbourhood of $100.00, and, as my first year's salary was only $100.00, I did not seem to see my way to such a purchase. But things turned out all right. In the Christmas packet Mr. Ross received was a letter from my father, enclosing a good big cheque to be used for my advantage in anyway, so long as it was not spent foolishly. Mr. Ross thought the dogs, harness, and carriole were useful articles, so soon I was the proud owner of some of the best dogs that could be found, and a harness to match. The outfit cost about $130.00. The Company profited by the transaction; I used them at all times on the Company's business, but they were mine and no one else was allowed to use them without my leave.

I spent my first Christmas day quietly. In the morning most of the inmates of the fort drove over to attend the service in the church at Rossville. I had been in the church several times before this and did not

Courtesy of the Glenbow Archives, NA–1408–7

Dog team and carriole at Fort Garry, circa *1872.*

feel very much interested in it, but on this occasion, there was a great change in the interior of the building. It was decked from ceiling to floor. Beautiful long streamers of evergreen hung from the high ceiling, and circles and crosses of the same decorated the walls and the ends of the long seats, and each high window was trimmed with ropes of green cedar.

For Christmas the church was filled to overflowing. The women had a quaint practice, I thought, when they attended the church. There were many large nails driven into the walls on either side of the building, and on these nails the women hung their babies during the service, tied up in their Indian cradles or "moss bags."

Native babies are generally very quiet and seldom cry, unless they are ill and pain makes them do so. The children of the Indian hunters, who spend most of their time in the bush, are taught from birth to be quiet because the parents think that any unusual noises tend to drive away any animals that may be in the vicinity of their camp. So if a child cries, and his mother thinks he is just crying for "cussedness," she promptly places her hand over the child's nose and mouth and shuts off its breath until the crying is stopped. Dogs in the bush were prevented from barking or

A Cree baby in a cradleboard.

howling by tying a leather thong round its muzzle, close to the nostrils. The ends of the thong were tied round the dog's neck so that it could not scrape it off with its paws.

The singing in the church this Christmas morning was good. It seemed strange to hear the dear old hymn tunes that I had heard from childhood sung to hymns in a language I was only beginning to learn. Indians, and more especially Indian women, have a good ear for music. Their voices are not strong, but they are very sweet and clear.

On New Year's Eve all the people in the fort at Norway House drove the two miles across the lake to the mission at Rossville where the Reverend E.R. Young gave us a fine sermon and lecture, pointing out to us the many events of the past year for which we should be thankful and exhorting us all to renewed efforts to "play the game" as God would have us do in the year that was now so near. A few minutes before midnight all hearts were bowed in silent thanksgiving for past mercies and prayer for help in the coming year to Him who alone can help us in all our troubles.

After the service, New Year's greetings were the order of the day, or rather night. The congregation was hardly out of the church when the kissing started. (I read these days in the papers how the Prince of Wales' arm and hand get sore from handshaking.) Well, it may be unmanly, it may be ungrateful, and it may be un-Irish to tell it, but I took and gave so many kisses that night that my lips felt numb for awhile, but in the morning I was ready to start all over, provided I was allowed to pick the ones that required to be kissed, which was no easy matter.

We all went back to the fort about one o'clock in the morning but had little rest. Everyone at the mission, and in and around the fort, seemed to be on the road, scores of dog sleighs with their jingling bells, and shouting drivers, passed up and down the river in front of the fort, and guns were being fired off in all directions.

I must have dozed for a short time after I got to bed but was soon awakened by someone in my room, close to my bed, saying in a loud voice "Goo-deal. Goo-deal. Oke masis." I got out of my bed to investigate. I had an idea that this was some New Year's prank of which I was not aware. The light in the room was dim so I lit my candle — no coal oil lamps in [those] days — and was rather surprised to see an old woman named Mary Jibb, a pensioner of the Hudson's Bay Company, who lived near the fort. She had made up her mind to be the first to wish me the compliments of the season and her "Goo-deal. Oke masis" meant "Good Year" and the "Oke masis" means in Cree "Young Master." I had to kiss the old girl, and she sat near the stove in the outer room to get warm while I got into my clothes. I gave her an order for some tea and sugar at the store and a plug of tobacco from my supply and sent her on her way happy. I found out later that it was the custom to make a present of some kind to the first one to greet you on New Year's morning.

There had been great preparations for the New Year in the kitchen at the fort for several days. Hundreds and hundreds of cookies, doughnuts, and many other sorts of sweet cakes had been baked and placed in large baskets and spread out on large tables in the officers' mess room in the "Big House." It was here that the officer in charge and his clerks met the people when they came to pay their respects. In this case, you could see the goodwill, and I may say, love in their greeting of Mr. Roderick Ross, the factor in charge of Norway House. He had been with them from childhood, with the exception of the years he had been at school and college in England. He was a graduate of Cambridge University.

As each visitor arrived there was handshaking and in case the visitor was a woman, she got the usual New Year's kiss. Each person was given a dozen or more cakes, or doughnuts, a small parcel of tea and sugar, and a plug of either smoking or chewing tobacco. In case of children, they were given the usual treat of cakes and a bag of candy "in lieu" of tobacco. At least six hundred persons passed in and out of the "Big House" that morning.

After dinner at the fort we all went over to Rossville to pay our respects to the Reverend Young and his wife. There was a good toboggan slide at the mission where we all enjoyed ourselves for a couple of hours, and there were also foot races for men and women, and dog races for others. The day ended with up with a football game between the fort people and the people of Rossville. The mission people got the worst of the game.

There must have been eight or ten different dances going on that night at Rossville and in the neighbourhood of the fort. I visited nearly all of them before morning. The principal dances were Scottish reels,

Reel of Eight, Reel of Four, rabbit dance, duck dance, and I must not forget the immortal Red River Jig. I tried to dance it that night, but I am afraid I was a failure, but several of my lady friends were kind enough to say that "on toward morning I could make my feet go pretty good," so I felt satisfied. "Rome was not built in a day."

I never heard the Red River Jig played the same in different parts of the country. Every fiddler has his own version of the Jig and they are all good. In the old days a fellow who could play the fiddle was looked upon as a blessing, no matter if he could only play one or two dance tunes. I remember asking a man at Slave Lake if he could play. He said, "Yes, plenty for make dance." I asked him what the names of the tunes were. He said, "One is the Red River Jig, the other isn't; don't know name, go dis way," and he started to move his legs and feet like the proverbial bear on a hot iron. He kept us dancing to his two tunes all night.

This was my first New Year's Day in the "Great Lone Land." It was my first away from home, though throughout the day I thought of home far, far away, I enjoyed myself. Still though, nearly at the end of "the long trail" and in the twilight of life, I can look back and have no regrets.

After the New Year celebrations, things at the fort settled down. Part of the time I spent in the office, the rest in the trading shop. I liked my work, but still I was glad when Mr. Ross told me he was going to send me to Nelson River Post to help the officer in charge there with the spring work.[4]

4 NATIVE MYSTERIES AT NELSON RIVER POST

*I*t was the middle of March [1873] before I left for Nelson River Post. The days were getting long and it began to thaw a little every day. We left Norway House early in the morning intending to camp our first night at Cross Lake, which was about forty miles away. The first fifteen or twenty miles of our trail was easy going because we did not have to put on our snowshoes. The Natives had been hauling fish over that part of the road all winter and the road was beaten hard, but in the afternoon things changed. The snow became soft from the heat of the sun making the rest of the day's run hard-going.

I was glad when we reached our camping place. I did not tell anyone I was tired, but I don't think I was ever so exhausted in my life before. I was not used to such a long walk on snowshoes. The wet snow stuck to them and made them very heavy. However, I made myself useful in getting our camp in order, cleaning away the snow, and cutting green pine boughs for our beds and to stick up to keep the wind off. The rest of the party were cutting dry wood and carrying it to the campsite. Soon our camp was finished and a fire started. The logs used for our campfire were about ten feet long and when the flames got going it was impossible to stand very close to it.

A big green log was placed on the ground close to the fire. This was used in the thawing of fish for our dogs. Of course, the fish were all frozen hard so they were stood up against the log to thaw. Each dog got three or

Courtesy of the Glenbow Archives, NA–1041–8

Cree trappers on snowshoes, from Picturesque Canada.

sometimes four fish for its supper, but the usual feed for a day on a long trip is one-and-a-half or two fish. These sled dogs were very patient and they sat around the camp in the snow waiting to be fed. They seemed to know that their meal was being prepared for them. We had sixteen dogs in our outfit, some of them strangers to each other, but there was no fighting or snapping at each other. After the dogs were fed they went a short distance from the fire and lay down quietly. I usually cut some green boughs for my dogs to lie on.

After the dogs had been taken care of, it was our turn to attend to the inner man. I was pretty hungry, but I was almost too tired to eat. I remember our supper consisted of pemmican soup, bannock, whitefish, and a very little salt pork. This we washed down with strong black tea with lots of sugar in it, but no milk.

I did not take long to get ready for my bed, and I soon lay down in my place in the camp and tried to sleep. I must have lain awake for hours. I found my feet too hot and sore. The rest of my body was cold, or at least I thought so. The men with me wore red woollen toques when they laid down. I had one and put it on, but found it uncomfortable and took it off. I then tried putting my head under the blankets, but thought I should suffocate and had to give it up. However, I finally slept and must have been sleeping for some time, for when I woke up I was very cold and the blanket, where my breath struck it, was white with frost and frozen hard. The fire was nearly out; only a few red coals remained of our once blazing logs.

I made up my mind to get up and start it going. The northern lights were shining brilliantly overhead and I could see everything around the camp quite plainly. Looking down towards the campfire, I thought I saw something lying near where my feet should be. I thought at first it was one of the dogs and spoke to it, but it did not stir. Then I tried to push it with my foot, but it did not move. Then I was sure it was some wild animal that might perhaps, when disturbed, show fight. So I drew my feet towards me for safety, but when I moved my feet this terrible animal moved towards me and I thought I was in for something. I was going to call to my companions but changed my mind and jumped up quickly. The beast vanished like a shot. Looking down at my feet, I saw at once that what had frightened me was my big lined buffalo-robe night boots that Mr. McTavish had given to me to use on the trip. I had forgotten all about them and did not remember that the hairy side was outside.

I soon got the fire started and warmed up and lay down once more, but only for, it seemed to me, a few minutes before the men were up, getting breakfast ready, and preparing for the road. I looked at my watch and found it was only four o'clock.

By five we were on the trail. My legs and feet were stiff and sore when we started, but the discomfort soon wore off and I felt all right, at least for a time. On these trips the custom used to be a rest for ten or fifteen minutes every two hours or so. And before evening, I was relieved whenever these "spells" arrived.

I was tired out long before camping time came. My snowshoes seemed to weigh fifty pounds each and the soles of my feet near my toes had become blistered from rubbing against the snowshoe netting. Altogether, I felt pretty well "all in," and I did not enjoy my supper and did very little to make camp. However, I slept that night. I was too worn out not to.

I went to bed dreading the next day, but it came, and I suffered as I did the day before, only ten times worse. I now had what was called "mal de raquette" or snowshoe sickness. I never felt anything like it in my life before. The cords up along my shin bone seemed to be twisted into knots and any movement of my toes made the pain a hundred times worse. My only comfort was, the men told me, that after a day or so, this pain would wear off when I became used to the snowshoes. The next morning I could hardly stand up when we were ready to start, but I knew I could not stay in camp alone. I managed to get under way after awhile and when I was warmed up the pain was not so bad.

That night we camped at an Indian's house at Scott's Lake. By now my feet were bleeding where the snowshoes caught me. The blood came right through my moccasins. Despite all I had a good supper that night. The man, in whose home we were camped, had been lucky and hundreds of pounds of moose meat hung from racks around the house. He also had a good supply of the meat of several beaver. He gave me a good supper of moose tongue and beaver, but I was too sore and weary to enjoy them.

The old man said he would try and help me get relief from the pain, and he did. He boiled some kind of roots in a pan and bathed my feet and legs in water as hot as I could stand. It did me good, but I still could

Fur trapper's cabin, from Illustrated London News, *May 15, 1880.*

Courtesy of the Glenbow Archives, NA–1406–292

not sleep and lay on the floor looking at the fire, wishing morning would never come. We were still three days from Nelson River Post. After a while the old man got up from where he lay and went outside telling me he would find something else to help me. He came back shortly with a little bag made of deerskin. He turned the bag out on his blanket to find what he was looking for, and, in a minute or two, came to me with what looked like a dried up rosebud. He told me to put it in my mouth, but not to chew it. He told me to lie down and I would soon be asleep. Shortly after I lay down again the pain in my feet and legs left me. I felt as if I had taken some kind of narcotic. My troubles passed away and I thought I was at home again.

I woke up next morning only after I had been called several times, so the men told me. Whatever it was, I felt no bad effects from it and the old man gave me two more of the little buds, one for each night that I would be on the trail. He told me not to say anything to my men. I gave him a suit of my underwear for his trouble and he seemed quite pleased. I have only run across this stuff twice, once at Lesser Slave Lake and again on the plains near Willow Bunch, Saskatchewan. I guess it has the same effect that morphine or cocaine has. I know, whatever it was, it helped out on the two following nights before reaching Nelson River.

We reached the post about dinnertime on a Sunday, five-and-a-half days from Norway House. I sat down to dinner and went fast asleep with my face in my plate. So much for my first long trip on snowshoes. In a day or two I was all right and ready for the road once more if necessary. It was my first and last trouble with snowshoe sickness. I have walked thousands of miles on them since but never had any difficulty of that kind again.

Nelson River Post was beautifully situated on a high hill overlooking an expansion of the Nelson River. The river at this point was about two miles wide and dotted with small islands that were covered with pine and spruce down to the water's edge. The water was clear and deep and some of the best fish in the country were caught here.

The Natives of Nelson River were the most primitive I had seen. There had never been a missionary there for any length of time and as far as I could see, they had all their old time superstitions and customs intact. It was at Nelson River that I came first in contact with the "medicine man" in all his glory and I found that he had a great influence upon the members of the tribe to which he belonged. They went to him for advice and depended upon him to tell them if they were going to make a good hunt or not. He was the one who officiated at the laying of the first timbers for a new canoe. It was he who told them the best places to make the fall fisheries, which they depended on in great measure for their welfare during the winter months. In that country, fish is what wheat is in civilization, and a poor catch of fish sometimes means starvation for people and dogs. The medicine man in many cases gave the children of the band their Indian names by which they were known through life.

In many countries that I have read about, these magicians seemed to be a useless lot who never worked for their living and obtained their livelihood through the superstition of their people. This was not the case with the Indians of the Canadian Northwest. To become effective as a medicine man and conjurer, he had to be a good hunter, a good provider for his family and near relations, always ready to help any of the band that were in trouble. His lodge was always open to the hungry who went there as a matter of course to eat at anytime, day or night. He was chief in more than name only. You could depend upon him and his promises. He was often pretty hard up because he gave all he owned to his friends and seldom got any return.

I became acquainted with two of these men during my stay at Nelson River Post and I saw them do things, that to this day, are a mystery to me. Not only did they do strange things, but they spoke of things that were to happen in the future, and in nine cases out of ten, what they said in their conjuring tent came true.

The chief at Nelson River in my time, fifty-two years ago (1873), went by the name of John Handy on the Hudson's Bay Company's books. He was the best hunter in that part of the country and was also a noted medicine man and conjurer. I feel it worthwhile to mention two noted examples of his powers of divination that took place while I was stationed at Nelson River Post.

The first winter of my stay at Nelson River was a very hard one for the Natives of the area. They had to go a long distance to find good hunting grounds, moose and deer being at that time scarce in the neighbourhood of the post. The snow was deep, three or four feet … and sometimes more. Those of the Indians, who were able to do so, went north and west to a distance in some cases of a hundred miles or more. Word had come that the deer from the North had arrived in thousands, so for a few days the activity was like what we call a gold rush.

The Natives came back to the post in the spring. They had had a productive time, lots to eat, and in most cases, a good quantity of furs. But some of the families belonging to the band did not arrive when they were expected, and their friends became very anxious regarding them. They waited for ten or fifteen days, but when the missing ones still failed to appear, John Handy was called upon to find out what had happened. So a medicine lodge was put up on the lakeshore, as near the water as possible, as old Handy told them that he expected to get most of his news from the Spirit of the *nisto-way-ak* or, in English, "[the] meeting of the waters." Three rivers met a little below Nelson House, and Nelson House is called *nisto-way-ah-seek* by the Indians " or "where the rivers meet."

At sunset old Handy entered his medicine lodge and began as usual to pray to his *Pow-ag-ons* or "too-tames" to let him know where to find the two missing families. He continued his prayers and incantations for an hour or more, then he was ready to talk. I shall try to tell as near as possible what he said:

> I see only one person where there should be five, I see the bones of three people. They are small bones. The living person is a woman, my daughter. I do not see my son-in-law. My daughter is coming this way, on the riverbank. She is very sick. She is dressed in rabbit skins. She is two days by canoe down river. Wait! Wait! I see her man going away from his lodge. He is going to hunt deer. The deer are like leaves, so many. He is far from home now. It is near morning. He is going to hunt. He leaves his camp and goes a little way and sees some deer. He takes off his snowshoes to get near the deer. His gun is not loaded where it lies near him. He is dead. He must have shot himself. It is snowing now. My daughter

cannot follow her man's road. My daughter and her children are starving. Soon I see only two children and soon again only one is in the lodge with my daughter. My daughter leaves the lodge. She is walking this way. She is carrying one child on her back. It is my oldest grandchild. My daughter falls in the snow many times. I see her walking again. She is not carrying anything. She is coming this way yet, towards the river. Her eyes look strange. Her hair is short. There is blood on her breast and arms. We must go and meet her. Someone must leave here at daylight and on the right-hand side of the river at noon he will find her. She can hardly walk. I am too tired to talk of Amis-koose tonight. Amis-koose will never come home, but I will find him.

Amis-koose and his wife were the other missing people.

One of Handy's sons and another Indian started off the next morning to hunt for the woman where Handy told them to look. And there they found her, more dead than alive. She was nearly insane and tried to run away when her brother approached. They had to tie her up in the canoe to prevent her jumping out and drowning.

When they brought her to the fort, she was able to tell part of what had happened, but for a week or so she was out of her mind and did not, or would not, tell a connected story. When she did speak at last her story was just about what the old conjurer had said it was. Her husband had gone off hunting and did not return to the lodge. After a day or two she left her three children in the lodge and went to look for him. A big blizzard came on and she lost her husband's track, and almost lost her own way back to her lodge.

There was very little food on hand at her lodge and she had a hard time getting even enough rabbits to feed the children. The youngest child got sick and died in a few days. Things went from bad to worse. Then the oldest child took ill and followed its younger sister. The poor woman had at last to leave her lodge with her only child, a boy about five years of age doing his best to get through the deep snow. But it was spring and the snow soon went, but the little boy had suffered too much and died before she reached the river.

I saw this woman every day until she died about two months after she was brought to the post. At times she appeared perfectly sane, but most of the time one could see that her mind was deranged. She was nothing but skin and bones and though she could not have been more than thirty or thirty-five years old, her hair was quite white in spots and her eyes looked like those of a hunted animal. I never found her crying. I don't think she could cry. There is reason to believe this poor woman had resorted to cannibalism before she left her lodge because some Indians who had visited the place in the fall found charred bones in the fireplace in the centre of the lodge which was still standing and there was no sign of any attempt to dig a grave and no dead bodies were found. The bones of this poor woman's husband were found later on, with his rusty gun lying among them.

Later on, John Handy said that Amis-koose and his wife had been drowned crossing a lake near where they had wintered, about sixty miles from the post near Burnt Wood Lake. And some of the Natives, who went there during the summer, found their lodge standing and the skeletons of two dogs outside. The dogs had been tied to sticks in Indian fashion, that is, a stick about two feet long, with a hole in each end through which is put leather thongs, one end is tied around the dog's neck and the other to a picket or a tree. Everything inside the lodge was in place. There was water in a kettle hanging over the fireplace and the bedding on the ground was undisturbed, so altogether it looked as if old Handy was not far wrong in his ideas of what had happened to Amis-koose and his wife. So far as I know nothing was ever heard of them again. Was Handy merely a good guesser? If not, who told him what was so near the truth. I don't pretend to explain it.

There were a few other old men attached to the Nelson River post who were supposed to look into the future and obtain results. One very old man, who was named Nah-tah-kam-ea-sew (in English, "Walking close to the shore"), had made a name for himself years before. He was called to his conjuring tent twice during my stay at Nelson River and both times he told what was going to happen or what had happened miles and miles away from the post. I shall only tell of one instance.

A man named Nah-tak-way had gone away to hunt deer and as he did not return when he was expected, the Indians began to wonder if anything had happened to him. A few days were given him to arrive and then the conjurer was called. Nah-tah-kam-ea-sew was the man chosen. His tent was put up close to the lodge of Nah-tak-way and soon our conjurer was busy. He said, "I see Nah-tak-way. He is in trouble. He is in a trap. He has been in it for many days. His leg is very bad but he is on his way home with the big trap on his leg. He is coming on the lake. Someone should go to help him. He managed to get to his canoe."

Soon a canoe was in the water and two men started off in the direction where they were told the man was to be found. That evening they returned with the man, more dead than alive, with the largest kind of bear trap closed a few inches above his right ankle. After getting him to his tent, the trap was taken off. He was in pretty bad shape and I thought he would be sure to loose his leg, but in a month or so he was able to get around pretty well.

He told me his story. He had set the trap close to the riverbank on a track made by the bears when looking for fish and on his way home in the dark had been careless and stepped into it. These traps weigh about twelve or fifteen pounds and steel clamps have to be used to set them, the springs being too strong to set them by hand as is the case with smaller traps. After being caught, he managed to get to his canoe and paddled back to his camping place for the clamps. He was going to change his camping place, and, as his leg had not yet become too painful to bear, he decided to wait awhile. He took up the clamps and tried to throw them into his canoe, but threw them too hard and they went over the top of the canoe and into the water. He was about five days paddling away from home so he was in a pretty bad fix. It is certainly wonderful what an Indian in those far back days could stand without the aid of a doctor and pull through. This man in a couple of months was as well as ever. Old Nah-tah-kam-ea-sew made a pretty good guess, eh?

In those days there was not much of what we call courting the girl you wished to have for your wife among the Native people. With them it was mostly a bargain between the younger man and the father of the girl. And the father, nine times out of ten, was like "Rou the Norman" [Rollo the Viking, an ancestor of William the Conqueror], and chose for his son-in-law the one who could give the most, and this sometimes caused complications, more so when one of the suitors happened to be a man much older than the girl he wanted.

While I was at Nelson River one such mix-up took place. There was, I remember, three competitors for the girl's hand and one of them was old enough to be her grandfather, but he was a rich man according to the Indian's idea of riches — hundreds of traps, many nets, many dogs, and more than all, being a first-class hunter, he had unlimited credit with the Hudson's Bay Company. The lady of his choice, however, was not after the riches belonging to an old man and besides, she had promised herself to a grandson of the old fellow who was trying to buy her. Old Min-a-Lake (in English "Spruce") paid over the goods to the father of the girl, and it looked as though a wedding and a big feast were about to take place, but they never thought of the lady's wishes or of the fact that she was in love with one of her other two admirers. The old man knew that his wife-to-be was in love with his grandson, but did not know of the third party, and that is where he lost out. The wedding was a few days away when the young man the girl had chosen was missing in the camp and everyone thought his heart was broken and that he could not stand to see the lady, whom he loved and who loved him, given to another man. We were all sorry for him.

The girl did not seem to mind his absence and went about her usual work, even cooking for the wedding feast and helping the other women and girls in the camp make some new dresses, the material for which had been given her by the aged admirer. Some of us thought the girl rather fickle, for she spent quite a lot of her time with the other young man who had wanted her, and at the Indian dances, she tried to get as near to him as possible, or stood facing him across the fire. Anyone who knew Native modes of lovemaking would be blind not to see that something was going on.

The night before the wedding day the bride and the young man slipped off in a canoe, and no one knew which way they went. The girl's father and the prospective bridegroom were raging, but could do nothing but speak of what they were going to do later, which did not help matters.

Old Min-a-Lake wanted his goods back, but did not get them at once because the girl's father said she might have been forced to go with this man and therefore was not her fault. Three days after the day set for the wedding the young man, who went away with the girl, returned to the camp and then we heard the rest of the story.

The girl and the man she wanted had made up the whole plan. He was to go away with his canoe and whole outfit as though he had given up all thought of the girl. Then he was to wait on an island in the Burnt Wood River until such time as she overtook him, along with the other man whom she had led to believe that she cared for and was willing to marry instead of the old man. She "drew the wool over his eyes" and he was more than willing to do all she wished him to do. So they left the camp together and she told him where she wished to go on their honeymoon trip. This was, of course, the place where she had told the other man to wait for her. She knew there might be trouble so on the way she took precaution to pour water down the barrel of the man's gun and also wet the priming, it being a flint-lock gun. When she and the man, who brought her from the camp, arrived at the island in the Burnt Wood River, where her lover was waiting for her, she pretended to be very much surprised, but said the least they could do would be to pay him a visit. When they pulled up to the shore, her lover's canoe was in the water at about the only place where a landing could be made, and it was all loaded ready to put out at a moment's notice. When the canoe in which the girl and her companion [sat] reached the shore, her lover stepped into his canoe as if to go away and not wanting to speak to either of them. Suddenly the girl stood up and jumped into her lover's canoe, which he quickly pushed from shore. The girl, at the same time pulled the other canoe with her, into the middle of the stream, and from a safe distance a treaty of peace was made. Our friend on the island was glad to get his canoe and other property back, minus ammunition for his gun for the return trip, because they could not trust him after he had been fooled so thoroughly.

This couple went through to Norway House and were the first Nelson River Indians who were married by a minister of a Christian church. They arrived at Rossville Mission on a Friday. So when the Reverend E.R. Young baptized them before their marriage, he called them John and Mary Friday. They seemed to be a happy couple. I saw them last at Norway House five or six years after their marriage. They had two nice little children, a boy and a girl. They elected me godfather for the boy, so I guess he must be all right.

At this point in the manuscript Halpin related his adventure at Cross Lake on the way back from Nelson River Post. It appears to be chronologically out of place and fits events of 1874 better than 1873. Therefore, the Cross Lake incident has been placed in Chapter Five. The Norway House Journal *shows Halpin arriving back at Norway House by boat on July 13, 1873, and resuming his duties there.[1]*

There were quite a lot of cattle kept at Norway House in those days, some to be used for beef in the winter. There were also several milk cows. I went to the camp where hay was made for those animals and it may be interesting to relate how the hay was put up. The grass for hay was cut along the lakeshore in hundreds of little bays and at the mouths of the little creeks that ran into the lake. All the hay was cut in the water with sickles. The water was at times up above the waists of the men who did the cutting. They cut an armful and went ashore with it and scattered it on the rocks where it dried.

This hay making continued until the water became too cold to work in. Then the hay was brought to the fort on York boats. Three or four boats were tied together side by side with strong timbers across them, thus forming a hay rack about thirty feet long and about the same in width. The boats could take six or eight tons at a time. About five trips were made for the hay, which had to be carried from the water's edge, by two men, the hay being placed on poles, something like a stretcher used in ambulance work. It came to me, in my work in the office, that this hay cost in the neighbourhood of fifty dollars per ton, if not more, but it was for "The Company."

Norway House was a pretty busy place that summer. There was hardly a week that some of the large brigades of boats from all over the country did not arrive at the post, either on their way from or going to York Factory. There must have been at times as many as a hundred boats tied up along the shore. Brigades came from McKenzie River, Athabasca, Saskatchewan, Île-à-la-Crosse, Lac la Pluie, Carlton, and Peace River via Fort Chipewyan.

Every northern and western HBC post had its quota of men in the different brigades and it is to the honour of the "Great Company" how easily they were handled. Here, men from different tribes met men whose fathers had been at war with each other in the past, but now, under the guiding hand of the Company, they were brothers and met with a hearty handshake and good will, the only rivalry being to see who pulled the best oar or played the best game of cards, or got the best in a gambling bout.[2] There were Sioux from Saskatchewan; Cree, Salteaux, and Assiniboine from the West; Chipewyan and Dog Rib and halfbreed Iroquois from the Athabasca and McKenzie River districts; and many a boat manned by French Métis from along the Red River and Lake Manitoba, and some from as far West as Qu'Appelle.

In the month of September [1873], I had a trip down to Oxford House, to the east about half way to York Factory. It was a very good trip lasting nearly three weeks.

I met the Red River brigade at Oxford House. They had twelve boats loaded principally with Hudson's Bay Company rum, which had been sent from England for use in the fur trade throughout the country. But as this liquor trade was now against the law, all the rum was shipped to Fort Garry, where it could be sold to people other than to the Indians.

There was a large supply of liquor at York Factory and the last of it was sent to Fort Garry in the summers of 1876 and 1877. It is to the credit of the boatmen on these trips that not one keg or barrel of liquor was broached or broken open on these trips of nearly five hundred miles of portages and rough country. I don't think white freighters would have done as well.

I passed the [...] winter, until the month of March, at Norway House, when I again went to Nelson River Post for the spring work.[3]

5 STRANDED ON CROSS LAKE

*A*fter getting through my work in the spring [at Nelson River Post in 1874] I returned to Norway House with two Indians in a canoe and had quite an adventure on the way. We had travelled as far as Cross Lake on our way home and camped for the night on an island in the middle of the lake. It rained nearly all night and the wind was very strong. We did not carry a tent on this trip and the only shelter was a canvas canoe covering about ten feet square, which hardly kept the rain off our blankets when we tried to sleep. The island where we camped was a small one with little wood on it. In fact, it was for the most part bare rock and moss. We put in a wretched night and intended to go to the mainland in the morning.

In the morning the rain continued to pour down and it got very cold. Sleet mixed with rain did not improve matters. It was towards the end of April.[1] About noon the wind died down, though the rain continued. So we organized our canoe and started for another larger island where there was plenty of shelter and lots of dry wood. We soon arrived there and made camp in the thick spruce timber and once we had a roaring fire going, all our late discomfort was forgotten. After a hearty meal, with copious draughts of tea, we fixed up our rain-soaked bedding and went to sleep. It cleared up in the evening, the sun stole from behind the clouds, and there was every promise of a fine day on the morrow when we expected to reach the end of Cross Lake.

In the morning we found that our troubles had only commenced. A little after sunrise one of the men went to the shore to prepare our canoe, ready for a start, but in a few minutes he returned to camp with the very bad news that our canoe was not where it had been left and was nowhere in sight. We all hurried down to the shore, and sure enough the canoe was gone. It must have been caught by the wind in the night and blown into the water. Now, what was to be done?

We talked the matter over and decided that our only chance was to build a raft and reach the mainland and follow its shoreline up until we reached the narrows where the Natives generally camped at this time of the year, fishing for sturgeon. This place was about sixty miles away as the crow flies from where we were, and we did not know how many miles it would be by skirting the shore, but there was no use in further talk. We had to act and at once because our provisions were running low, though that did not make much difference as we had our guns and plenty of ammunition, so there was not the slightest danger of our going hungry.

We soon went to work and early in the afternoon had a good trustworthy raft built. We had to tear up our canvas canoe cover to make ropes to hold the raft timbers together, so our prospects, if it started to rain again, were not too bright once we completed our raft. The wind was fair for reaching the place we wished to land on, and though it was late in the day, our head canoeman decided it was safe to start. The mainland was about six miles from where we were, and, if we had luck, we should reach there in four or five hours. We put up a sort of mast on our raft and used our blankets for a sail.

So off we started, and for an hour or more made good time, hoping to get across the lake before dark, but our lucky star grew dim. The wind went down and there we were, nearly in the middle of the lake. The water became quite calm and the drift of the water was in the direction from which we came. We were soon heading back to our starting point. Night was coming on and a cold drizzle of rain added to our discomfort. We had been trying to reach the eastern shore of the lake, but an hour or so after dark the wind started to blow from the east. We could not see the island that we had started from, and it must have been not far from daylight when we struck shore on the western side of the lake. There was nothing for us to do but wait patiently for a change of weather.

We had a kind of "Scotch fine weather" all night and we were soon all well-soaked. There was plenty of wood where we landed, but everything was wet, and, as we had no matches, it took some time to get a fire started with flint and steel and touchwood. This is easily done in fine weather, but in the dampness it was a different thing.

At last the fire was started and we dried ourselves, had a good meal, and, as usual, forgot our troubles. Eventually, we sat down to think what was best to do under the circumstances. To travel on the western side of the lake was out of the question. Our head canoeman said it would take a week to reach the narrows. I left the men and went off in the afternoon and managed to kill three ducks and a large jack fish, which I shot in a swamp where he had gone and had become trapped. Of course we had a fine supper and went to bed in a rather contented frame of mind, notwithstanding the bad fix we were in.

In the morning the weather was fine and the wind was from the West. So off we started, once more heading across the lake. We reached the island where we had camped the day before, had dinner and tightened the canvas ropes on our raft, which had loosened up quite a bit during our voyage. After dinner the wind blew very strongly, so much so that it was not quite safe to trust ourselves on the raft, so we had to stay where we were, and there we did stay for three long days and nights.

We might have stayed much longer had not a couple of Natives from the narrows happened along on one of their hunting trips. They were Norway House men, and were carrying plenty of food, dried sturgeon, and other things to eat. They told us that our canoe had been found on the east shore of the lake opposite the island where we camped. There were no paddles in it. They must have fallen out when the canoe was blown into the water.

As not all of us could get into the small canoe that these men were using, my head canoeman returned to the east shore where our canoe was found while the other man and myself remained on the island until his return the next day. I shot a wolf that night. It was a timber wolf and

Courtesy of the Glenbow Archives, NA–4405–19

Fur traders near Norway House.

I was quite proud of myself. The skin was not prime, but I used it for several years as a mat in my bedroom.

A few hours after sunrise the man who had gone for our canoe returned and we started from our island after a delay of nearly five days. That night we slept at the Indian's camp and headed out for the narrows next morning. We arrived there safely that evening.

There were a large number of Indians camped at the narrows as it was, at that time, one of the best sturgeon fisheries in the country. There I met for the first time that noted missionary, the Reverend James Settee (later Archdeacon).[2] He was on his way to establish a mission and school for the Indians somewhere on Cross Lake, wherever a suitable site for buildings could be found. The Reverend gentleman's large family were travelling with him, along with a number of men who had come with him to help put up buildings and start the cultivation of some land in connection with the mission. We camped with them that night and left early in the morning to continue our journey to Norway House.

About noon that day we camped for dinner at what the Indians call the "Painted Stone." This is near the southern end of Cross Lake. The lake narrows here to a width of about two hundred yards, surrounded on both sides by rocks about one hundred feet above the lake level. The rocks on both sides of the lake look as if at some time in past ages they had been joined together and that some great convulsion of nature had split them in two and placed them where they stood. The rocks are straight down from top to bottom and look as though a cat would hardly find a foothold on the face of them. But some human being must have been on the face of those rocks at sometime or other, either from top or bottom, because they were painted in different colours with life-size figures of men, moose, deer, dogs, birds, and canoes. This painting must have been done hundreds of years ago, for the oldest Indian I ever spoke to on the subject told me his grandfather told him that his great-grandfather had told him that the painted stones were old when he was a boy.

At that time I could see marks on these rocks made by the waters of the lake at different times, but no mark within thirty-five or forty feet from where the paintings were. Whoever did the paintings must have been lowered from the top of the rock. The work must have taken many days to do for the pictures show great care in execution. How these paintings have stood so long without washing off has always puzzled me. The pictures were not cut into the rock, but were simply crude paintings of things familiar in the everyday life of an Indian. The colours used were blue, red, and yellow. Perhaps someone will be able to tell us more about these in the future. The Indians say a big bird let Wee-sug-ah-chak stand on this back while he did the painting, Wee-sug-ah-chak having helped him out of a snare some time before.[3]

Two days later we arrived at Norway House and I settled down once more to my usual work in the office and trading store.

In September 1874, I received orders to proceed to Oxford House. I was sorry to leave Norway House. I had had a pleasant time there and both Mr. and Mrs. Ross treated me as one of their family. I was still a boy and missed my home surroundings, and I had come to feel a great liking for Mr. Ross and his family. Going from one Hudson's Bay post to another in those days only meant changing houses, for one got a hearty welcome wherever one went.

Chief Factor Roderick Ross's assessment of his distant relative (Halpin) was quite different from what Henry Ross Halpin imagined. The following evaluation was written by Ross on September 8, 1874:

An apprentice postmaster @ £20 per annum and now completing the last year of his first contract. He is a town-bred Canadian lad with a very deficient education, of reckless habits, and I am afraid bad principles. For some time I considered him incorrigible, but latterly he has begun to improve a little in his behaviour, and he has also made some slight advance in acquiring a knowledge of the business. He is as yet, however, so unreliable that he requires the closest supervision. So far, he has been of very little use to me, but with what he has now learnt, he might be utilized in some more remote District where opportunities of playing the fine gentleman and temptations of a disreputable tendency would not be so distracting and irresistible as they are here.[4]

6 Oxford House

I left Norway House with the fall packet for York Factory late in October [1874][1] in a canoe with two men, and I enjoyed the trip. The mosquitoes had left the country until the next summer. Water fowl of all kinds were plentiful on our route and the scenery in some parts of our trip was simply grand. Streams, white with foam, rushed along through cliffs, and here and there were beautiful waterfalls whose thunder swelled and died away in this lonely land. High cliffs and higher mountains meet the eye at every turn of the river, down which we were travelling at a rate of two or more miles per hour.

The woods along the shore have changed from their summer green leaves to the most beautiful tints of autumn: gold, red, all shades of orange, pink, and purple. In fact, there seemed to be hundreds of different colours. A bear was standing by the side of the river hunting for fish and at our approach did not seem to be frightened, but walked off slowly up the steep bank of the river.

The greater part of the country between Norway House and Oxford House seems to be mostly rock and muskeg, but there are some long stretches of open prairie-like land, which, I suppose, will some day be settled and homesteaded by some land-hungry person. Fish swarm in every river and lake and, in the past, wild fowl of all kinds were there in their thousands.

Part of our journey was made over a route not used by the York boats as in some places the streams we navigated were hardly wide or deep enough for our canoe to get through. At other places over which we carried our canoe were waterfalls and rapids in which no boat could live for a moment. Our journey being downstream all the way, we made good time and reached Oxford House on a Sunday evening, four days out from Norway House. York boats generally take seven or eight days.

I was met at the door of the "Big House" by a gentleman with a long flowing beard, a grand-looking man. He was dressed in what looked like a clerical set of clothes and when I addressed him as Mr. Sinclair[2] I discovered my mistake. He told me that Mr. [Cuthbert] Sinclair was out somewhere, but would shortly be in, and that he was Reverend [Orrin] German,[3] the Methodist missionary from Jackson Bay Mission. He held divine service every two weeks at the fort.

I came to know Mr. German very well during my three years' stay at Oxford House and found him to be a fine man in every respect. At that time he was a bachelor and his home was wherever he happened to be. Later on he married a lady schoolteacher from Norway House. She was a sickly woman and she died a few years later at Calgary, Alberta, where Mr. German had been sent in the course of his duties. Poor Mr. German died shortly after his wife, somewhere near Vancouver.

Mr. Sinclair came in shortly and after supper we talked far into the night over a glass of nice hot toddy made with Hudson's Bay rum at least seventy years old. I will tell how this nectar happened to be on hand.

Mr. Sinclair was going to build a new dwelling house and was going to place the building over the site where an old trading store had stood for at least fifty years. When the men, who were cleaning out the old cellar, reached the bottom, they came across an old eighteen-gallon oak keg. The wood was in capital shape and did not appear to be damaged in any way. When they pulled it out of the earth and rubbish, where it had lain for a generation or more, it was found to contain at least ten gallons of the very best rum, at least seventy years old. It was a prize all right. Mr. Sinclair and I had a little of it at times for about two years. It was used only on state occasions. The Reverend Lachlan Taylor, inspector of missions for the Methodist Church in the North, pronounced it "good" on several occasions during his stay at Oxford House.

Courtesy of the Glenbow Archives, NA–2749–30

Oxford House, Hudson's Bay Company.

After I had settled down in my new home, I took time to explore in the neighbourhood. Oxford House stands on a high hill facing Oxford Lake, a body of fine clear water, about thirty miles long and from five to ten or fifteen miles broad. Hundreds of islands dot the lake from end to end and the water is so clear you can see the bottom ten or twelve feet below the surface. Some of the finest whitefish in the country are caught here and lake trout of large size are plentiful. Some of these fish, which I have seen, weighed up to eighty pounds and were four or five feet long. These fish are not often caught in nets, hooks being used for the purpose.

The Indian name for Oxford House is *Pie-e pow-nipee* or "Hole in the water" in English. Not very far from the fort is a small arm of the lake about a mile and a half in circumference, bounded by high wooded hills. This piece of water is entered from the main lake through a narrow channel hardly twenty yards wide and not very deep, but after you enter the little bay or lake, the water suddenly deepens until no bottom can be reached. I tried to reach the bottom with about five hundred yards of stout line to which I had attached weights of lead. I did not succeed. This "hole in the water" was a fine place to enjoy fishing with rod and line, and sometimes in summer I used to get my dogs into a skiff and row to this place and get enough fish in half an hour to give them all a good feed.

Oxford House is one of the oldest Hudson's Bay posts in the country. I saw diaries written by factors in charge of Oxford as far back as 1808, and in some of a later date was an account of the passing up to Red River Settlement of the "Selkirk Settlers."[4] One contingent of these hardy Highlanders rested at Oxford House for nearly a week on its way from York Factory to what is now Winnipeg. Some of these people tried to reach Fort Garry by an overland trail in the winter, and when I went over this same road in the year 1875–76, some of the log shanties put up by these settlers were still to be seen, or rather, the ruins of them. Several of the stone and mud chimneys were still in a good state of preservation and are perhaps still standing. I think a party of English soldiers also came over this road in the early part of the last century.

There was a fine garden at Oxford and about twenty acres of other land under cultivation. Barley and oats were grown that were equal to any grown in Manitoba today.

There was a camping ground at the foot of the hill along the lakeshore near the fort, and it was a favourite resting place for the brigades on their way to and from York Factory. The boatmen, if possible, tried to get here for Sunday, which was generally a day of rest on these long tiresome trips, and they all enjoyed the one day's diet of splendid whitefish and trout that they were sure to get at Oxford. This helped the Natives belonging to the post as they were able to exchange their fish and dried meat for tobacco, tea, sugar, and flour, with which the voyageurs were well supplied.

During my second summer at Oxford House I saw a pretty good fight on the beach between an Oxford House man named François Savoyard. He was a very big strong fellow and fully six feet tall. (Years before he had come from somewhere in the Red River country and married an Oxford House girl and settled there.) The other man, Baptiste La Roche, came from, I think, Fort Qu'Appelle. This was not one of the championship fights, but a private quarrel of some kind. Both men meant business and if the fight had been allowed to continue, either one of the men or both would have been killed.

They fought for over an hour, biting, kicking, scratching, and gouging. Savoyard had been able to get a good grip on La Roche; he could have choked him to death, but La Roche was light on his feet. He would kick Savoyard anywhere he liked and be five feet away the next minute. Savoyard bit off a nice piece of La Roche's ear, and La Roche pulled handfuls of hair from Savoyard's curly head. At last La Roche knocked Savoyard off his guard, pinned him on the ground, and broke four of his ribs by jumping on him.

This ended the fight for that time, but a year or so later Savoyard came across La Roche in Red River. La Roche was drunk and at once renewed the old feud, but this time, Savoyard was the winner, and La Roche was laid up in the St. Boniface hospital for some months with a broken jaw and other minor injuries. Savoyard was one of the strongest men I ever saw. I saw him push a York boat that had been pulled up on the sandy beach, into the water. This is pretty good work for four men. Not surprisingly, he was a mighty eater.

During my stay in the Oxford House district I had "winter charge" at God's Lake Post, and, while there, I was visited by Savoyard, who came to trade.[5] It was about Christmas time so I told my man to give him something besides fish for his meal. My servant made ready a good meal of moose meat and pickled pork enough for two men, besides a good-sized bannock. Savoyard put away the whole business without trouble, and, as I was anxious to see what he really could do, I told my man to heat up some smoked whitefish, which I had on hand. He ate the four fish placed before him and still looked hungry. Then my man said, "Let me give him some dried apples." I was a little afraid, but I told him to go ahead. So Mr. Savoyard topped off his meal with about a pound of dried apples. He slept at my house that night and I could not see that he suffered the slightest inconvenience from this monster meal. He drank about a gallon of tea with the aforesaid meal. I have heard of some Native men being able to eat twenty pounds of fresh meat in a day, and I believe many of these strong men could do so without any trouble.

7 The Legends of God's Lake

*I*n my time very few Native families made their headquarters at God's Lake. The place had a bad name. A few years before I lived there an epidemic of measles carried off most of the people living around the lake. The disease had been brought to that country by evil men[1] from the Red River settlement. Men, women, and children died almost daily until more than seventy people belonging to the post were gone, and, from what I heard, I wonder any of them remained alive to bury their dead. The disease reached them during the summer and I was told that when the spots (or rash) were at their height and the fever more than they could stand, they would go back into the muskeg, carrying their children with them, lie down on the cool wet moss and cover themselves over with it at the same time, and of course death was not far off when that sort of cure was chosen.

One day I went to the Trout Falls to fish. I had two men with me and made a good catch. At noon I went for a short walk around the falls and came upon fifteen well-made graves. Upon asking my men who were buried there, they said that they were the crews of two boats from Red River who were overcome with measles on their way to York Factory. They also used wet moss as medicine for their trouble and died, one after another, until only two were left out of the original seventeen men who made up the crews of the two boats. These two men stayed with their comrades and buried the last one before leaving the place. They "played the game," eh?

It was during my stay at God's Lake that I had my first experience in hunting and trapping beaver in winter. I went off with three Indians to a place were they said beaver were plentiful and that we could take along plenty of traps to set for other animals while we were breaking into the beaver houses, which they said would take some time and was very hard work. So off we started with two teams of dogs and a good camping outfit. It took the best part of two days to reach our destination. We made a comfortable camp and spent the next two days in setting traps and snares in the neighbourhood of the beaver lodges. And then the real purpose of our journey began.

In the first place we collected a lot of dry wood, which we placed on top of the largest beaver house. We kept the fire up all night and by morning we had the big beaver house composed of logs, stones and mud pretty well thawed out. Then we set to work to cut away the ice around the house to find out where the doors leading into it were located.

This beaver house was one of the largest kind and the Indians were sure there must be a dozen or more beaver wintering in it. Three doors were found about three feet under the water. Two of these were blocked up by driving posts into the bottom of the lake in front of them, and in

Courtesy of the Glenbow Archives, NA–843–23

A sketch of a beaver village, from Canadian Pictures, *drawn with pen and pencil by Marquess of Lorne, Governor General of Canada, 1878–83.*

94

the third hole, a trap was set. Then two of the Indians and myself started to cut our way into the beaver house with axes and ice chisels. This was pretty tough work, but before we had worked very long, the man who was watching the hole where the trap had been placed, pulled out a large-sized beaver, killed it at once, and set the trap again. Five more beaver were caught before we got into the lodge. Four more were speared or killed with an axe before we quit for dinner. The top of the beaver house was now covered over with pine brush and a few heavy logs placed so as to keep it down and make the place as dark as possible. The trap was removed from the hole and everything left as far as possible as we found it.

After dinner we went through the same performance at another beaver house that was found not far away. There were seven beaver houses in all that we wanted to break into, so we could not hurry.

In the morning we built fires on three of the largest houses and then we all went to see the traps we had set on the day of our arrival. Only one of us had much luck. Pierre caught three fine fishers and two marten. The two other men got a few mink and a lynx.

I snared a mink and a marten. I also found a place where an otter had been working under the ice in a small stream that ran into a small lake not far away. I set a trap in the water in this creek under hanging ice. This was my first attempt at trapping in this way, having only been told by the Indians how it was done. I must have made a good job of it because I got the otter when I visited my traps two days later.

We again gave our attention to the beaver houses and broke into six altogether, catching thirty-two beavers during the nearly nine days we were away from the post. The first lodge alone yielded twelve. I thought we did very well.

It was on this trip that I had my first view of the interior of a beaver house and it was a very interesting sight. The walls of this large house averaged three feet in thickness. On the top it must have been more. The inside of the house was quite dry and clean and was composed of peeled poplar logs, of all dimensions, from an inch or so to six or eight inches in diameter. The interior of the house was about four feet high in the middle. The beaver lodge itself was about six feet in diameter. Four families of beaver had lived there and you could see where each family

Courtesy of the Glenbow Archives, NA-843-23

A Cree family at God's Lake.

had made its beds, which were composed of dry grass and moss. The floor was clean and white and there were three holes in the floor of the house near the walls. The water did not come within three feet of the floor of the house. The place smelled like a brewery.

After we had broken the dam and let the water out, we could see where the beaver had stored their winter supply of twigs and green poplar sticks. The poplar sticks were standing nearly upright in the mud in deep water, ten or fifteen yards from the lodge and could be easily pulled out by the beaver when wanted for food. The ice in the dam was about three feet thick, and, after the water was run out, it hung for an hour or so before falling to the bed of the stream. The area covered by the water in the dam must have been two or three acres in extent.

Manitoo Sa-ke-hay-gan (in English, "God's Lake") gets it name from an Indian story that is as follows:

> Many years ago, before white people came to the country, a family composed of a father, mother, and seven children, all boys, but one, came to camp there in the summer and things did not go well and many times they went hungry. The father tried his best to procure food but failed.

One night the youngest of the boys had a dream. When he got up in the morning he told his father and the others that he thought he could get food if he tried. The father did not want him to go away alone, but the boy persuaded him to let him go and try his luck. The boy went off and never returned to the lodge, but he was not dead because the canoe, which he used on his trip, was pulled up on the shore near the camp and in it were eight large trout, one for each member of the family still left.

After this the other five boys had dreams similar to that of the youngest boy. They went away but never returned to their lodge, but they always sent tokens to show they were still alive.

Then one night the father had a dream and next morning, before his wife and daughter awoke, he left the lodge, paddled out into the lake, and waited to see what would happen. He was far out in the middle of the lake, four or five miles from shore. Not having had a good night's rest, he went to sleep in his canoe and when he awoke, he found that he had drifted alongside of what he took to be a rocky island. He thought this strange because he had never seen this island before, but he was going to step ashore and stretch his legs. So he stood up in his canoe and stepped out on what he thought was a rock, but no sooner had he done so, than it sank under him and he found himself in the water. In a minute or so after he was seized by a monster trout and swallowed. And there, inside this monster fish, he found his six sons all alive and uninjured so far as he could see.

Shortly after he had seen his sons the fish moved to the shore near the camp and pushed the canoe up on the beach, then it turned around and swam into deep water. After a while it swam between some very high white rocks where everything was bright like day. The light came from what looked like a [star.] The big fish now opened its mouth and the father and his six sons were made to walk out and they found they were in a beautiful lodge, which was covered with large butterfly wings. The place was full of flowers and thousands of butterflies were flitting from flower to flower.

Some very large butterflies flew to where the father and his sons were sitting, and each butterfly had a large clam shell full of honey and wild rice on its back between its wings. The boys and their father were hungry, but they could not finish what was placed before them.

After they had eaten, a beautiful hummingbird came and perched on the father's knee and began to speak as follows: "I am not what I seem to be. I am not a bird, though I am a beautiful one. I was once a man like you, but a bad spirit changed me. When I was a young man I loved a beautiful girl, the daughter of a great chief and she loved me, but a bad man also loved her and he got a medicine man to try and kill me. The medicine man had pity on me, but wanted the bad man to think I have been killed. He was afraid to let me live as a man, so he changed me into a hummingbird and threw me up in the air so I could fly away. We were near the lake when the medicine man tried to make me fly, but I did not know how to use my wings and the big fish swallowed me when I fell into the water.

The medicine man told me I should remain a bird until a man and his wife and seven children, one a girl, should come to the lake to camp. The big fish was to tell me when they came and help me to get the girl with the father's consent. She was to come in the same way that her father and brothers had come, through a dream, but she could not have the dream unless it was the wish of her father, and if he did not consent, he and his sons were to remain where they were forever, and his wife and daughter would perish from cold and hunger."

The father then spoke to his sons as to what should be done, and one after another gave his consent. The next morning the big fish went out to the middle of the lake to wait for the girl in the canoe and about noon she paddled out. She had trouble getting away from her mother, who did not want to let her go. As soon as she stepped upon what she, like her father, thought was a rocky island, the canoe was overturned and she was soon in the inside of the big fish which at once swam away to the butterfly lodge. She was soon with her father and brothers and her father told her all that had taken place and, though she was afraid, she said "For my mother's sake I will remain with the hummingbird for he is beautiful and will never hurt me."

No sooner had she spoken, than the hummingbird flew towards her and lit on the ground near her feet. She stooped to lift it up, but when she put her hand out to take the bird, it was gone and there before her stood a handsome young man who held out a hand which she took at once.

The butterfly lodge then rose to the top of the water and they found themselves on a beautiful grassy island and a large canoe was tied to a tree close to the shore. There were no paddles in it, but the young man, who had been a hummingbird, told them all to get into the canoe, which they did. He then told the girl to put her hand in the water, and, as she did so, the big fish rose to the surface and getting behind the canoe, pushed it towards the shore. When they were halfway between the island and the shore the young man told the girl to hold her hair up in the air, and, as she did so, the island sunk out of sight and thousands of beautiful butterflies were in the air where the butterfly lodge had stood.

They were now close to shore and the girl was once more told to put her hand in the water, which she did at once. The big fish was swimming close to the canoe as she raised her hand from the water. The big fish could not be seen and in its place stood the medicine man who had spared the life of the young man and watched over him so long. That's the story of God's Lake....

I remained at God's Lake Post until open water and then left for Oxford House, taking the fur I had traded during the winter, and also the balance of the outfit [supplies and trade goods] I had brought along in the fall with me. It took three good-sized canoes to hold our furs and goods. We arrived at Oxford House without any trouble.

8 York Factory

Although Henry Halpin was assigned to Oxford House, Hudson's Bay Company correspondence shows that he was sent to York Factory on Hudson Bay early in 1875.[1] The request for his going to York Factory had come from James Fortescue, the chief factor at York Factory, who had written to Cuthbert Sinclair on February 10, 1875: "I hear that you have Mr. Halpin staying with you and as I am hard pressed for assistance in the store during the packing season, I shall be obliged if you would lend him to me for the spring, to come down with the spring packet, and I would send him back to you [with the] first boats."[2]

Cuthbert Sinclair communicated the request to his superior Chief Factor Ross at Norway House, and passed along his evaluation of Henry Halpin:

> With regard to Mr. Halpin I must say he has been of some service in the way of assisting in the Indian shop whenever the Indians come in, and is ever willing and ready whenever called upon. I think with a little careful training something might be made of him as an Indian trader. I don't think he will ever make an office manager judging from the dislike he has to the desk. I would be very glad to have him in the District and give him a fair trial. No doubt he will be of some use with want of opposition coming down this way to take charge of

parties sent out amongst the Indians. He is acquiring the language fast which will be very useful to him in the trading with the Indians. Mr. Fortescue, being short of hands, has applied for him to assist in packing [?] I intend sending him down along with the packet men on their return. I hope he will give satisfaction.[3]

Halpin's former boss at Norway House wrote back to Sinclair: "I am glad for his own sake that Mr. Halpin goes to York Factory. Tell him that he has now an excellent chance of getting his name up and no doubt if he behaves well and gives satisfaction, he will be permanently retained at York Factory and will get on."[4]

The summer passed without any event worthy of notice and I was glad when, late in the fall, orders came for me to be sent to York Factory soon as possible after winter set in. So about the middle of November 1876[5] I started off with two teams of dogs and two men on my way to York Factory. The snow was not deep as yet so we made pretty good time. We left Oxford House on a Monday morning and delivered our winter "packet" to Mr. Fortescue, the officer in charge of York Factory on Sunday evening, seven days from Oxford House.

It was about nine o'clock in the evening when we arrived. Of course, we were expected, but even so, our arrival caused considerable excitement. When you get letters from "home" only three or four times a year, you want them badly when they arrive. I was taken to the "Big House" at once, had fine warm bath, and good supper, and then went to the office to see the "packet" opened and the mail distributed.

There were, I think at that time, nearly two hundred Hudson's Bay Company employees at York Factory.[6] Most of them were Orkney men.[7] It took more than an hour to get through sorting and delivering the mail, and then things in the Post Office settled down for another five or six months. Every old country man, I think, received letters from home that time, so they were happy. Mr. Fortescue, Mr. R. Mills, Mr. Mowat, and J.K. McDonald, second in command at York Factory, sat up nearly all night reading the "news" from old country papers nearly three months old.

Courtesy of the Glenbow Archives, NA-3694-2

An aerial view of York Factory.

J.K. McDonald, mentioned above, was a fearless hunter, and had several polar bears to his credit before he left York Factory. At the time of his death in Winnipeg some years ago, he held a commission as chief factor in the Hudson's Bay Company.

After resting for a few days after my long trip, I was given work in the depot, superintending the packing of a large quantity of merchandise, which was to be sent to Red River during the coming summer. I was kept pretty busy, but still I had plenty of time to look around both outside and inside the fort.

York Factory was a small village within itself. I think there must have been eight or ten acres enclosed within the stockade. All kinds of trades were carried on and the place, even in winter, was full of life. In those days most of the ironwork for the whole country was done at York, such as traps, axes, ice chisels, rat spears, chains for traps, etc. There were carpenter shops, cooper shops, sail makers, boat builders, and box makers. All the packing cases for the whole country were made there, as well as all kegs and barrels.

There was a lot of work done at York in the winter. All merchandise came from England in large bales, barrels, and boxes, weighing in some cases, half a ton. All these different pieces had to be opened at York and packed over, in bales or boxes weighing not more than eighty pounds each. Moreover, all the fur that had arrived during the summer from all over the country had to be opened and repacked into bales of five or six hundred pounds each. Then, from inland, would come bales of musquash [muskrats], containing five hundred furs; they were now packed into bales, which contained five thousand or more. Every bale of fur, buffalo robes, isinglass [a very pure form of gelatin obtained from the swim bladder of a sturgeon], and feathers, etc. were opened and sorted and all damaged fur was put to one side and packed by itself.

The principal building at York was the "Northern Department Depot." This building was, I think, about two hundred yards long and a hundred yards wide, and three storeys high. It contained everything as we used to say, everything from a nail to an anchor.

York Factory was built on a swamp, or nearly so, but as the ground never got a chance to thaw out for more than two or three feet down, buildings, which had been built fifty or sixty years before, were not an inch out of plumb. The depot faced the river and along each side and behind it, were the other factory buildings. A broad boardwalk ran from the main door of the depot to the front gate overlooking Hayes River and in the middle of the boardwalk stood a sun dial placed there by Sir John Franklin on his last visit to York Factory.

All of the old buildings at York Factory were of much interest to me, but none could take the place of the office. Here you could find shipping bills from England one hundred and fifty or more years old, with quaint Old World wording and strange writing. I read some letters over one hundred years old and schedules from the directors in London dictating the prices to be paid for the different kinds of fur. There was a very fine library at York Factory and many of the books, first editions, could not be obtained at any price today.

The Church of England had a mission at York under the charge of the Venerable Archdeacon Kirkby. The church, in which he held the services, was made of iron and had been sent from England in the Hudson's Bay ship, in pieces, ready to be put up. It was very comfortable and had good furniture also sent from England.

Archdeacon Kirkby had lived in the McKenzie River District before coming to York Factory. (He left York and went to the United States and died in Rye, New York State, many years ago.) He was a small man, not more than five feet high, but he made up for it in girth, and must have weighed over two-hundred pounds. He was a fine man and his wife was "one of the best."

The ships from England could not come up the river to York Factory, but had to cast anchor at the "five fathom hole" about fifteen miles out from the fort.[8] From there the cargo had to be brought up the river in schooners, lighters, and York boats. Hayes River is shallow and the tide runs like a millrace. At most times the water is rough.

When the ship arrived in the fall, all hands at York turned out to unload it and for two or three weeks it was a kind of holiday at York, though hard work was the order of the day. But it was a change and people like a change. Sometimes when the weather turned bad, the ship had to

Courtesy of the Glenbow Archives, NA–1041–7

Loading and unloading cargo at York Factory. From Picturesque Canada, *circa 1882. Cargo from ocean-going ships had to be off-loaded onto small boats first.*

pull out into deep water and wait until the storm passed before the men could get the cargo all unloaded or load on the furs, etc. from the fort.

The weather is very uncertain at York. I have been almost driven mad by mosquitoes in the morning and before night it would be snowing and the river covered with ice floating from the bay, driven by a north wind. There was a snowstorm of some kind, large or small, every month during the summer I spent at York Factory.[9] This happened almost every time the wind came from the north, especially if it was inclined to rain, which almost always turned to snow.

It was simply wonderful, the amount of merchandise stored in the depot, and it took months to pack it in bales, boxes, and barrels of such size and weight as could be handled on the portages between York Factory and Norway House. There seemed to be about fifty portages between these two places, some of them half a mile long.

The depot was a department store in every sense of the word. Everything that one could wish for in those days could be found there and in large quantities. Up to this time the Hudson's Bay Company sent everything for the trade for the whole country, including Red River, to York Factory. Now they found that most of the requirements for Saskatchewan, Alberta, and the Far North, Athabasca, and McKenzie River districts, could be brought in cheaper through the United States via St. Paul and down the Red River in steamboats from Moorehead, Minnesota. This was the reason for shipping all surplus stuff from York, and only enough was kept there to supply the outposts on the Bay and a few inland posts attached to York.

I did quite a lot of hunting during the winter months and in the spring game of all kinds was plentiful close to the fort — white and red foxes, wolves, wolverine, and mink. In the spring we were given a holiday for two weeks to go to the Beacon Point at the mouth of Hayes River to hunt geese. I never saw so many waterfowl in my life before. Geese of all kinds were there by the tens of thousands. It was a wonderful sight when the tide was out to see the geese, ducks, and swans on the mud flats along the bay. When the tide was out, these flats were bare for three miles out from shore and this was the feeding place. I have seen this whole place covered with white geese or "wavies" as we called them. The place looked like a prairie covered with snow. The wavies came in before the tide and we used to make hiding places with spruce boughs and from there did our shooting. Fifty or sixty geese in a few hours was a general thing.

The Hudson's Bay Company used to engage some marksmen from among the Homeguard Cree [those Cree who lived around the fort and supplied labour to the Hudson's Bay Company] to shoot geese for them. Hundreds of barrels of geese were salted down for winter use. About thirty geese were put in each barrel and some men would fill four or five barrels a day. They were supplied with free ammunition and were paid about a dollar per barrel for the geese. The wives and family of the hunters did the plucking and sold the feathers to pay themselves for their work.

I visited the men hunting porpoise at the mouth of the Hayes and Nelson rivers, and found it a very interesting sight. The manner of hunting porpoise by the Natives is as follows: When the tide is out and the water low, they find a place where there are mud banks not too far apart and where there is deep water when the tide is in. Across the lower opening between these mud banks they drive strong stakes or pickets into the bottom of the river. Then they twine strong ropes or branches of willow in and out between these posts until it looked like a big basket. It is made very strong. At the upper side of the passage they put up a strong stage, which will be five or six feet above the high tide. All they have to do now is to wait for the porpoise to appear, which does not happen every day, but when they do arrive in the river, our man is already on his stage ready for business. The porpoise come in by hundreds from the bay on their way up the river, up which they go for at least thirty miles or more. A porpoise, when shot in the right place, sinks like a stone to the bottom of the river and this is where our hunter has use for his basket or net at the bottom of the river…. The porpoises will sink and roll in the direction of his net, and, when the tide goes out, if he does not find five or six porpoises in his basket, he is not satisfied.

White whale are also hunted in this manner, but they are rather risky customers to deal with, and, while at York Factory, I heard of one man being drowned when an eighteen-foot whale, which he only wounded, knocked his stage down. He missed getting hold of his boat, which was tied to the stage, and with no one being near enough to help him, he was swept out to sea.

The present site of Fort Nelson is about twelve miles from York Factory across the point of land between the Hayes and Nelson rivers. This portage was in my time a good place for deer and more than once my dogs chased them for miles. One evening near the Nelson River I saw more than three hundred in one flock [sic]. Ten or fifteen were common.

One morning in spring while I was there, a flock of deer, fifteen I think, came in at the back gate of the fort with about fifty husky dogs at their heels. It was a fine sight to see the deer jump the six-foot fence in front of the fort and make off across the ice on the river. None were killed as everyone was taken by surprise.

There is a lot of talk these days regarding Nelson River. In the winter when I was there,[10] it was not until Christmas when the river froze over. The men from Churchill had to go twenty or thirty miles up river to find solid ice to travel on with the winter packet for Red River. The Hayes and Nelson rivers were open in the middle of May in the year [1875] I was at York and at times clear of ice, but when a north wind continued for a day or two, even in June, ice could be seen in both rivers.

The river at York Factory is about four miles across to "Ten Shilling Creek" where there is quite a settlement of old Hudson's Bay employees. There is fine trout fishing in this creek, and I spent many a night there and caught some good bags of trout. In June and July we had plenty of light to fish all night.[11] The only drawback being mosquitoes, which were there by the billions, I think.

The shores of Hayes River are well-wooded. Of course, most of the large timber had been cut down during the more than a hundred years since the Company had settled there. The river is full of small islands or rather sandbars, which often change as to size and shape.

Hayes River is shallow, and, when it flows hard, it is not a good place to be in a small boat. An old man and myself were caught once between "Beacon Point" and York Factory. The tide was running out and we were driven before a strong north wind. The tide runs eighteen miles up Hayes River and is only stopped by a ten-foot waterfall at that point, even porpoises went up with the tide that far. It was after dark and we could not see far, when suddenly we ran into a big tree, full of branches, which was floating down stream. Our boat almost turned over and we were carried about four miles down towards the bay before we got out of our entanglement. It was daylight before we got home where I found Mr. Fortescue, officer in charge and others, who had been anxious about us all night.[12]

Nelson River at the mouth is, I think, about twenty miles broad or perhaps a little more. On a clear day one can see the opposite shore quite distinctly, but most times it cannot be seen. I know very little about the mouth of the Nelson. It was rather far to travel to hunt and the waters of the bay were generally too rough for small boats.

The Hudson's Bay Company got all their boat timber and hay from about one hundred and fifty miles up the Hayes River at a place called by the Indians *Sa-ma-ta-wah* River, which is a branch of the Hayes. The hay was loaded on large rafts of boat timber and floated down to tide water, eighteen miles from York. Then the rafts were tied up to the bank until high tide and then run over the falls. They hardly ever lost either hay or timber.

Twenty head of cattle were kept at York Factory — about six cows and the rest were work oxen used for hauling fuel in winter. It took a lot of firewood to supply the needs of the inmates of York.

There was not much chance of being lonely at York Factory during the winter. Most of the employees were married men and dances and parties came off two or three times a week. The dances were held in the carpenter shop, which was a large building. Three or four sets of Scottish reels and such dances could be on the floor at the same time.

We also had winter picnics in the woods miles from the fort. These picnics used to be great fun. Nearly every man at the fort had a good team of dogs and a carriole, and I have seen as many as thirty teams of dogs at some of these turnouts. The snow was all cleared away and several big fires were kindled. Then the men of the party started off with their guns to hunt. An hour and a half was allowed for their return and the man who made the best hunt received a prize of some kind from the lady who had accompanied him. This prize was generally a pair of fancy gloves, neck tie, or moccasins. Any game, like rabbits or partridges, was dressed and cooked at the big fires and eaten on the spot. We had singing and, if not too cold, musical selections played on the bagpipes by several pipers who were among the employees at York. Of course the journey home was a race and the dogs enjoyed the trip as much as the drivers.

This is the end of Halpin's larger manuscript. In late June 1875, Henry Halpin was sent back to Oxford House. Chief Factor Fortescue noted in a letter to Cuthbert Sinclair on June 10, 1875: "Mr. Halpin, who has assisted as far as he could, will be returned to you by your own boats as you may have need of him during the coming summer."[13]

On June 28, 1875, he sent Halpin off: "Mr. Halpin takes passage by the same Brigade for return to Oxford. He was useful to us during the packing season, but I have no employment for him further, and York is not a place where it is good for a young man to have nothing to do."[14]

9 POSTMASTER

*B*y the spring of 1875, Henry Ross Halpin had completed his period of apprenticeship. In May of that year, Commissioner J.A. Grahame wrote to Cuthbert Sinclair: "I have no objection to your keeping [Halpin] with you, trusting that you will give him the careful training which you think will eventually make him useful as a trader."[1] Following the meeting of the Hudson's Bay Company Council, Halpin was raised to the rank of postmaster and again assigned to Oxford House.[2] Grahame informed Sinclair of Halpin's promotion: "Mr. Halpin is left with you for another year according to your recommendation of him and I hope to get good account of him next season. Encourage him to make himself useful and keep me advised of his behaviour."[3]

With the position of postmaster came added responsibilities for Henry Halpin, one of which was to supervise the staff when Sinclair was away and keep the daily journal of the post's activities. Hudson's Bay Company daily journals usually commented on the weather, the comings and goings of personnel, and significant events. Compared to the reports prepared at York Factory, Cuthbert Sinclair and Henry Halpin's entries for Oxford House were very detailed and sometimes they used the daily log as a personal journal in which they revealed their anxieties and very personal attitudes.[4]

One of the main concerns, which springs from the Oxford House Journal, was the constant need for food to feed themselves, the Native and Métis staff, the dogs, visiting boat crews, and Native traders who came *to Oxford House. Another thing that stands out was the antipathy that Cuthbert Sinclair had for Native people. Even Halpin found some of them difficult, particularly the Native women who hung around the fort.*

This chapter contains Henry Halpin's journal entries, but Sinclair's comments about Halpin's activities have also been included in this chapter because they illustrate the variety of work he was doing at Oxford House. The prefix [Sinclair] identifies Sinclair's entries.

August 24, 1875: "Very warm today. Blowing a little from the SE. Busy giving advances to the tripmen. Three boats start for L[ake Winnipeg] tomorrow. Mr. Sinclair goes with them as far as Norway House. Wm. Grieve still working on new house. Three boats hauling hay. Old Billy Moar attending the nets; only 4 whitefish and 9 suckers from the nets this morning."

August 26, 1875: "Cloudy but very warm, with light showers of rain during the day, but not enough to prevent the boats starting ... Have been busy debting[5] some Indians that are getting off. The sooner they go off the better for everyone that has anything to do with them."

August 27, 1875: "Continual showers of rain all day. Bad weather for haymaking. Three boats hauling hay from the back lake. I got the Indians that I gave debt to yesterday off today. I was beginning to think I was [stuck] with them until Mr. Sinclair returned, but they were not quite away when Savoyard arrived from Norway House and also Robert Bee from the Trout Fall. I gave him a few supplies and he will be off tomorrow. Savoyard will have to wait until Mr. Sinclair returns from Norway House for his debt, as there is no flour to give him ... Old Billy attending the nets as usual; poor haul of fish: only 5 suckers and 3 whitefish from ten nets. If we do not get more fish soon we will be short of flour before the boats arrive...."

August 28, 1875: "I gave Savoyard a little debt this morning. He is going to the Trout Fall to live the best that he can until Mr. Sinclair comes back from Norway House. I gave Edward Robinson his debt this evening with the exception of flour...."

August 29, 1875: "Mr. German held divine service three times today. I attended twice. The Island Lake canoe arrived this morning for a few supplies required by Mr. Linklater for the trade. I will try and get them off on Tuesday...."

August 30, 1875: "Raining all day. Wind from the SW. Very bad weather for hay making. There is a great deal of our hay spoiled as it has been so long on the ground, but I cannot help it as it would not do to put it in a stack when it is wet. The York Factory men arrived from Norway House this morning and gave me the Packet. I gave them provisions to York. I do not know whether I did right or not. Only 6 whitefish from the nets this morning...."

August 31, 1875: "Still cloudy and damp. Several showers of rain fell today. I am thinking all our hay will be spoiled ... I was fitting up the Indian's shop, with the goods that I took out of the bales that I had to open for the Island Lake men. I took a haul with the seine net in the narrows today and to get some fish (as the calls on me for something to eat at all times of the day is a little too good for the flour to last long), but I did not catch anything. I will try again tomorrow. Nothing like trying 'if you want to succeed.' "

September 1, 1875: "Still cloudy and damp. It was very warm, just the sort of a day to spoil the hay. Edward Robinson started for his hunting grounds this morning. Still no boats from York although it is long past their usual time to arrive...."

September 2, 1875: "Fine warm day. Just the day that I was waiting for the hay. We got most of it put up in cocks and ready to stack on Saturday if the weather permits ... Joseph Day arrived this evening from Jackson Bay where he is building a house. Reports that he cannot get enough fish for one meal a day. We are as badly off here in the way of fish."

September 4, 1875: "The York Factory men came this morning for provisions as they had none ... I do not know what I will do if the boats from Norway House do not turn up soon. I have only two bags of flour and also [there] is every chance of the boats not coming for a week yet. Some of the York Indians arrived this evening. They brought in a little fur, which they gave me. I wish that Mr. Sinclair were at home

AT THE PORTAGE.
Hudson's Bay Company's Employés on their annual Expedition.

Courtesy of the Glenbow Archives, NA-1041-6

Hudson's Bay Company voyageurs at a portage on their way to York Factory. From Picturesque Canada, *circa 1882.*

as he would know how to get on with them better than me under the present circumstances. Only 10 suckers and 2 whitefish from the nets this morning. I made Wm. Ray set some nets out in the front lake today as perhaps we might get a little more in the way of trout which have appeared. (Hope so.)"

September 5, 1875: "... Two Red River boats arrived this morning with some provisions which [were] badly wanted. Still no fish, although we have twelve nets in the water. We only got 15 suckers and 2 whitefish this morning. Mr. German held the usual services today. The attendance was better than usual owing to the number of men about the place."

September 6, 1875: "... Only 3 suckers and 4 whitefish out of twelve nets. If the provisions had not arrived when they did we would have been starving soon. I wish for my own part that Mr. Sinclair was back as I am not used to giving out provisions at the present rate."

September 7, 1875: "... I do not think that I have enough hay 'but I have my orders' so I must obey them as far as it is in my power ... Wm. Ray attending the nets but getting nothing worth mentioning. Only 4 whitefish and 1 sucker this morning. The calls for charity in the way of something to eat is something awful, but it is hard to refuse as everyone knows that it is a bad thing to be hungry."

September 9, 1875: "Snowing and raining all day. It is going to freeze hard tonight ... We got a better haul of fish this morning: 9 whitefish, 5 trout and 14 suckers. A lot of Indians arrived today from God's Lake with a little fur which they gave me. I think all the hay is gone to the land of nod...."

September 10, 1875: "Beautiful bright day, wind from the SE. Mr. Sinclair arrived from Norway House about 4 o'clock p.m...."

September 13, 1875: "... Mr. Sinclair and myself busy all day debting some Indians that are waiting to get off as soon as possible and the sooner they get off the better as they are a bother ... Ray attending the nets. We are getting a little more fish now: 19 whitefish, 15 suckers and 2 trout from the nets this morning. I hope the fish will increase as it will save the flour and pork."

September 15, 1875: "There was a hard frost last night and it has been very cold all day. Debted a few Indians in the forenoon. Four Indians arrived from Trout Lake this afternoon. They brought in a lot of furs. They are the dirtiest lot of men that I have ever seen. They beat the Nelson Indians *re* being dirty and the Nelson River Indians are dirty enough."

September 18, 1875: "… I gave myself a cut in the leg with an axe this morning which will keep me quiet for a few days."

September 21, 1875: "… The place looks very lonely now that all the Indians are off. Mr. Sinclair thinks their absence is good company."

October 1, 1875: "Mr. German arrived from Norway House this afternoon. He left Norway House last Sunday. The new steamboat was there for one day. Treaty made with the Norway House Indians by the Canadian government. They have given each Indian $5 and $25 to the chiefs…."

October 5, 1875: "… Mr. German held divine service three times today. I attended twice. It will be a year tomorrow since I left Norway House. It seems a very short time…."

October 24, 1875: "… As Mr. German is not here, of course there was no service in the church. I think Sunday is the longest day of the whole seven because I have nothing to do on Sunday, but think."

November 18, 1875: "Old Billy and Ray attending the nets: 69 whitefish and a few sorts from eight nets. All the rest of the men were employed as butchers. Old Tom, one of the oldest oxen, about 15 years, was killed today. He is in very good order. I expect that he will weigh about 800 lbs. at least. We moved into the new house, bag and baggage today. The house that we were living in before was getting too cold."

November 23, 1875: "… Mr. Sinclair and myself visited our traps this afternoon but as usual got nothing."

November 25, 1875: "Poor old James Grieve got himself badly burned last night. It appears that he got up in the night and [laid] down beside the fire. Some of the sparks flew out of the fire and fell on his shirt which ignited, and before anyone knew anything about it, the shirt was all burned off him, except a little bit on the right shoulder and the neck. Poor old chap. I think he is nearly played out."

November 26, 1875: "… Old James Grieve died this morning about daylight without a struggle. He must be about eighty years old. He has been about 60 years in the service of the Company. He will be interred tomorrow."

December 6, 1875 [Sinclair]: "… Mr. Halpin and Joseph Hart left this morning for John Wood's camp with two trains of dogs."

December 11, 1875 [Sinclair]: "… Joseph Hart and Mr. Halpin arrived [back]…."

December 18, 1875 [Sinclair]: "Mr. Halpin went out to the Mission this afternoon. He will be back tomorrow…."

December 21, 1875 [Sinclair]: "… Mr. Halpin and Joseph Hart started for the other end of the Lake to see the Indians [that] hunt in that section of the country and [to] secure the furs that they have collected since winter set in, and likewise to bring home some rabbits if any up there…."

December 23, 1875 [Sinclair]: "… Mr. Halpin and Joseph Hart arrived from the *Wapanapanis* with some fur and 40 rabbits…."

December 29, 1875 [Sinclair]: "… Mr. Halpin made a trip to the "doorway" and returned this evening with 320 whitefish…."

January 3, 1876 [Sinclair]: "… Most of the Indians left for their homes and I am not sorry for it, having been trouble the whole week."

January 15, 1876 [Sinclair]: "… Mr. Halpin met with an accident today, having fallen down stairs in the shop when going up with some furs. He feels his back very sore in consequence, but [I] hope nothing serious…."

January 17, 1876: "Quite warm for this time of year. In fact it came very near raining this morning. Mr. Sinclair started for Island Lake Post with three men. He will be off about two weeks. James Moan and Joseph Hart accompanying him. I do not think he could go very far today, as it has been [so] soft underfoot. The dogs would soon get tired out…."

January 18, 1876: "Weather much the same as yesterday, but I think by the look of the sky this evening we are going to have it cold, which will be a good thing for Mr. Sinclair who is off on his break … I began to give the men [dried] fish today, [because] if we keep on giving out the fresh ones, we will come out at the wrong end of the horn in the spring."

January 22, 1876: "Joseph Chedly arrived from Jackson Bay Mission bringing 3 [minks] 'which were not his own.' He is one of the most useless fellows about Oxford House and I think it would pay the Company if they gave him something to stay away from the fort…."

January 23, 1876: "John Mason is still on the sick list, but I don't think it is a very serious malady as he can eat as much as anyone about the fort. There is one sure proof of an Indian being sick and this when he is not able to eat. As far as I see, John is not very bad."

January 24, 1876: "… I did not give the Indians that came from God's Lake much as they are not trying to pay their debts. In fact, one of them by the name of 'Wenesk' got nothing as he had not killed even one mink the whole winter … Mr. Sinclair will have started from Island Lake this morning. If so, I expect that he will be here on Thursday or the day following. All the females that came to the fort yesterday are off, thank goodness, for they are a bother about the place."

January 25, 1876: "Joseph Canada came from the 'clay banks' this evening. He has been off for about ten days after deer, but did not succeed in killing any. While he was off he fell in with Old Jacob Hart's party and he tells me that they are starving having nothing but rabbits to eat and moreover they did not know that the trains from the Fort had visited their camp, so they were out of two things that an Indian thinks it is impossible to live without, viz. Tea and Tobacco. But no doubt, now that Joseph has informed them of the fact that both articles are to be had at their old encampment, they are 'drinking and smoking to their hearts' content.'"

January 27, 1876: "… Mr. Sinclair arrived from Island Post this afternoon. All well in that quarter, but they are getting very few fish."

January 29, 1876 [Sinclair]: "… James Moar and Mr. Halpin went to the winter fishery for some fish; brought home over 300 and there is some there yet."

February 29, 1876 [Sinclair]: "… Mr. Halpin and myself went for rabbits at the [?] called the Bridge. Returned in evening with 100…."

March 9, 1876 [Sinclair]: "… Mr. Halpin and James Moar started for the *Wapanapanis* for rabbits with two trains of dogs…."

March 24, 1876 [Sinclair]: "York Factory Packet left for Norway House, Mr. Halpin accompanying it…."

April 4, 1876 [Sinclair]: "… The Red River Express arrived, Mr. Halpin likewise returned from Norway House along with his Reverence O. German…."

April 5, 1876 [Sinclair]: "The Red River Express left for York Factory. Mr. Halpin working in the Indian shop putting things in order…."

April 6, 1876 [Sinclair]: "… Mr. Halpin and old Billy left with two trains of dogs going for the meat of two deer…."

April 8, 1876 [Sinclair]: "… Mr. Halpin and old Billy arrived with over 300 lbs. of venison."

April 27, 1876 [Sinclair]: "… Mr. Halpin and myself moving the goods into the new trading shop…."

May 23, 1876 [Sinclair]: "… Mr. Halpin and myself taking the inventory."

May 26, 1876 [Sinclair]: "… John Mason assisting Joseph Hart planting potatoes in the garden. Mr. Halpin and myself sewing some small seeds. Fish scarce, dogs starving like rats."

These journal entries give us a window into the day-to-day life that Halpin and others in northern Manitoba experienced. His romanticized image of the fur trade was being replaced by the realities of harsh subsistence.

10 ISLAND LAKE POST

*T*he relationship of twenty-two-year-old Henry Ross Halpin with his supervisor Cuthbert Sinclair had been souring for some time. In a letter written in 1885, Halpin complained that he had been the victim of abuse by traders McTavish and Sinclair ten years earlier. He did not indicate whether this was sexual harassment by the older men, but he said that they played "some tricks more dirty than usual on me." When his complaints to Chief Factor Roderick Ross went unheeded, he reported that he became disheartened, gave up, and no longer tried to please his masters.[1]

After the end of May 1876, Halpin's name was absent from the Oxford House Journal for several months with no explanation. It is possible, but not certain, that he spent some more time at York Factory.

Sinclair's journal entry in the Oxford House Journal on July 3, 1876, was the last one before he went away that summer. On that day he also wrote to Commissioner Grahame at Fort Garry. One of the major things on Sinclair's mind was the possibility of free traders providing competition in his area: "I am glad to state no opposition reached this [area] to date, but will probably be down sometime in the summer, and I am given to understand [they] intend establishing themselves permanently somewhere in this vicinity, and will most likely establish a fort at God's Lake, being the most profitable place for fishing in the surrounding county, in which case, it will be necessary to re-establish the post out there, which will necessitate some competent person to take charge."[2]

One might imagine Henry Halpin being considered for the position since he had already spent time at God's Lake, but Sinclair ruled that out: "Mr. Halpin, I must say, is incapable for the position and [I] would certainly not recommend him. He does very well to assist in trading with the Indians and is very useful in sending on trips in the winter, but to put him on his own at a post would be an injurious step."[3]

During the summer of 1876 Sinclair did not leave Halpin in charge at Oxford House as he had done before while he was away during previous years, but instead transferred Thomas Linklater from Island Lake Post to Oxford House and sent Halpin to the remote Island Lake Post to replace Linklater.[4]

It is not clear when Halpin left for Island Lake, which was situated about eighty miles southeast of Oxford House. Strangely, there were no Oxford House Journal entries from July 4–8, 1876. Linklater arrived at Oxford House on July 9 and began making his own journal entries. He was immediately confronted with starving boat crews.[5] On July 29, he noted in the journal that he had received word that "Mr. Halping [sic]" had arrived safely at Island Lake.[6]

Because the journal for Island Lake Post no longer exists, we can only piece together Halpin's summer experiences there from other sources. Cuthbert Sinclair arrived back at Oxford House on September 25, and Linklater left for Island Lake on the next day.[7]

On September 28, Sinclair sent Billy Moar and an Indian named James to Island Lake to get fish and presumably to accompany Halpin back to Oxford House. The journal entries reflect Sinclair's concern when Billy Moar did not return on time, but no concern was shown about Halpin's welfare.

October 6, 1876 [Sinclair]: "… no sign of Young Billy Moar returning from Island Lake. No doubt this weather is detaining him. I hope they won't get frozen in."

October 9, 1876 [Sinclair]: "… I begin to feel anxious about Young Billy Moar. He ought to have been here some time ago. He has, fortunately, got a very good Indian that knows the country along with him and if they have got any ammunition (which no doubt they have) they will hunt [on] their way. I was in the same fix myself 10 years ago coming from the same place with the same Indian. [We] got frozen in and [were]

Courtesy of the Glenbow Archives, NB–40–8

Island Lake Post, Hudson's Bay Company, in 1909.

obliged to walk across the country. Such misfortunes frequently happen in this country...."

October 14, 1876 [Sinclair]: "Young Billy Moar arrived along with Mr. Halpin from Island Lake. They got frozen in at the high hill portage. [They] left the canoe there and walked across the country, leaving everything behind. All well at the outpost, unfortunately catching very few fish...."

The journal contained very few items about Halpin's subsequent time at Oxford House. One of the significant events was the collapse of the huge rack on which fish were being dried and frozen.

November 2, 1876 [Sinclair]: "Our stage for fish gave way last night and fell down to the ground with over 9,000 whitefish...."

November 3, 1876 [Sinclair]: "... Donald McKay and Mr. Halpin employed carrying hay into the barn...."

November 4, 1876 [Sinclair]: "... others hauling up the fish from the stage. Got most of them into the ice house in old store...."

November 27, 1876 [Sinclair]: "… Young Billy Moar and Donald McKay returned this morning with the goods etc. that were left at the high hill portage last fall…."

December 2, 1876 [Sinclair]: "… Sent Donald McKay and Henry Ross Halpin to the winter fishery for fish and rabbits. Returned with 100 whitefish and 50 rabbits…."

December 4, 1876 [Sinclair]: "… Donald McKay and H.R. Halpin cutting fire wood at the Little Lake…."

The disintegration of the relationship between Halpin and Sinclair appears to be reflected in the two last cited journal entries. He was no longer referred to as Mr. Halpin, but as Henry Ross Halpin and H.R. Halpin, the way an angry parent might address a child.

The mails were slow and when Commissioner Grahame answered Sinclair's letter of July 3, 1876, on December 12, 1876, he wrote: "Should you find it necessary to re-establish at God's Lake, under the circumstances you explain, you must get assistance from Mr. Ross who no doubt can […] lend you some reliable trader until one can be procured elsewhere. I regret that Mr. Halpin, after the experience he has had, is still unfit for an independent charge."[8]

A letter which Sinclair wrote to Commissioner Grahame on December 17, 1876, sheds more light on that issue: "… I regret to say that he [Halpin] is incapable of taking charge of an outpost, judging from the careless and extravagant way affairs have been conducted during the last summer in Mr. Linklater's absence at Island Lake Post. With respect to the affair of managing, he made another attempt on my return to raise the subject."[9]

Sinclair's unhappiness with Halpin seems to have intensified after the Island Lake Post furs and remaining trade goods had been retrieved from the portage on November 27. His reference to Halpin's "careless and extravagant" methods at Island Lake might suggest that he was giving more than "good measure" to the Natives in exchange for their furs. Halpin's "extravagance" may have been an attempt to compete with the free traders, a practice that had historically been employed by the Hudson's Bay Company, but now in a tighter economy may not have been used as much.

Sinclair may also have felt Halpin was "too generous" in providing food to the hungry Natives at Island Lake Post.

Courtesy of the Glenbow Archives, NA–1406–46

A trapper on his rounds, from Harper's Monthly, *June 1879.*

11 OFF TO THE NORTHWEST

In December 1876, Cuthbert Sinclair told Henry Ross Halpin that he had been ordered to send him to Fort Garry for reassignment. The Oxford House Journal *made no reference to Halpin's departure, but he apparently left on December 18 when the York Factory Express arrived from York Factory.[1]*

Halpin travelled with the dog teams on their way to Norway House, carrying the damning letter that Sinclair had written to Commissioner Grahame the previous day, along with other mail for Fort Garry. The temperature was -30° F.[2] He arrived at Norway House on Christmas Eve[3] and remained there until January 6, 1877.[4]

When Henry Halpin and his travelling partner Lambert arrived in Fort Garry on January 23, 1877, there was great confusion. There were no known orders for Halpin to come to Fort Garry. Chief Factor J.H. McTavish exchanged a hasty set of telegrams with Commissioner Grahame who was at Grand Forks, North Dakota, on his way to England. "Lambert and Halpin arrived. All well. Where is Halpin for?"[5] Grahame replied, "Know nothing about him. Letter should explain."[6]

Unfortunately, Sinclair's letter did not explain, nor had any other correspondence on hand indicated, that Halpin was to come to Fort Garry. Sinclair had merely said, "According to your instructions Mr. Halpin now takes his departure for Fort Garry...."[7] That the instructions might have been oral from an earlier face-to-face meeting between Sinclair and Grahame appears unlikely because of Grahame's ignorance of the matter.

The Company officers at Fort Garry were left in a quandary. Had Sinclair acted without explicit orders? Not wanting to bother Grahame further while he was on his trip, J.H. McTavish sent Halpin to the Swan River District pending the commissioner's return from England.[8] The Swan River District, to which Halpin had been sent, extended from Lake Winnipegosis into central Saskatchewan and included Fort Qu'Appelle. In another letter G.M. McTavish specifically stated that Halpin had been sent to Fort Qu'Appelle.[9]

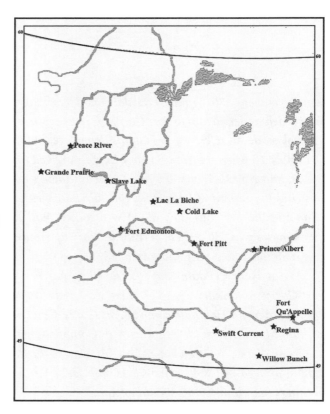

Places Associated with Halpin's Fur Trade Career in Saskatchewan and Alberta.

After Commissioner Grahame returned to Fort Garry in May 1877, he did not criticize Cuthert Sinclair, but noted: "Mr. Halpin arrived here during my absence and was sent to another appointment before I returned. It is very much to be regretted that some young men will not endeavour to merit the approbation of their employers, and the character [reference] you have given of Mr. Halpin is such as leads me to consider him quite unsuited for the service, and unless a more favourable report is made of him this summer he will be discharged."[10]

When the Council of the Hudson's Bay Company met during the summer of 1877, it listed Henry Ross Halpin among those clerks and postmasters who would "be permitted to retire."[11] At the same time he became a "freeman," working in the Swan River District for the Company. Personnel records show that he maintained that relationship with the Company until 1878.[12]

On October 6, 1878, Henry Halpin's father died in London, Ontario, after suffering a paralyzing stroke.[13] Even though the funeral was delayed for a week, it is not likely that Henry would have been able to get the message and return home to be with the family because there was no Canadian railway running from the West at the time. He would have had to travel by steamboat down the prairie river systems to Lake Winnipeg and go south to North Dakota to get the closest train to Ontario.[14]

Henry Halpin's movements between 1877 and 1884 are shrouded and his relationship with the Hudson's Bay Company is unclear. He claimed to have traded buffalo hides at Swift Current in 1877. He was also at Willow Bunch, a settlement halfway between Moose Jaw and the United States border. At the beginning of his longer memoir he stated that he engaged in fur trading as far west as British Columbia, and family tradition had him even working in the Mackenzie Valley. His memoir also stated that in 1880 he was at Lac la Biche in northern Alberta. He also mentioned being at Lesser Slave Lake. The 1881 census listed him as a trader at Peace River. His immediate neighbours were Hudson's Bay Company employees and Catholic clergy.[15]

One of Halpin's letters from 1885 sheds light on his movements during that shadowy time after his unfortunate experience at Oxford House. "Mr. Grahame told me that I was dismissed and I expected no less at the time. I was out of the service for nearly four years and then I was taken back by Mr. James McDougal, chief factor, at Peace River who gave me charge of a good post, Grande Prairie. I did very well during the time I was there, but when Mr. Grahame heard that I was there he sent orders to have me dismissed again, so I had to leave a second time. Well, last fall I met Mr. McLean who was in charge of Fort Pitt [near the Alberta/Saskatchewan border] and as he knew me for the last thirteen years, he gave me employment again."[16]

And so by the fall of 1884, Henry Halpin was again in the service of the Hudson's Bay Company, managing its post at Cold Lake in northeast Alberta. He reported to William McLean, the chief trader at Fort Pitt, and established a friendship with Big Bear, a Plains Cree chief, whom he regarded as a "good" Indian. On occasion he had stayed overnight in Big Bear's tent while travelling between Cold Lake and Frog Lake.

The tumultuous events of the Riel (or Northwest) Rebellion (now being called the North-West Resistance) in the spring of 1885, would directly impact Henry Ross Halpin and propel him onto the historical stage. The "rebellion" was the result of protests by starving Natives and landless English and French Métis, and angry white settlers in Saskatchewan objecting to federal government inaction and expressing their own desire for provincehood. They sought help from Louis Riel, a Métis lawyer who had negotiated the terms for the creation of the province of Manitoba in 1870.

Courtesy of the Glenbow Archives, NA–382–1

A group of Cree men at Fort Pitt in the fall of 1884. Big Bear is on the right.

Riel returned to Canada from exile in the United States and took up their cause. He drafted a petition for provincehood that was sent to the federal government. Riel's presence met with government opposition and police harassment that ignored their legitimate grievances. The situation was compounded by the fact that Riel, who suffered from periodic bouts of mental illnesses, had grandiose plans for the Northwest and the rest of Canada where he would be prophet, priest, and king.[17] When the federal government ignored Riel's demands, he created a provisional government, established a Métis army, and seized the government stores at Duck Lake, taking several hostages. The conflict was exacerbated by the reckless activities of a North West Mounted Police officer, Leif Crozier, who ordered his men to charge a group of Métis led by Gabriel Dumont , at Duck Lake, Saskatchewan, on March 26, 1885. The Métis returned fire and a dozen police and volunteers were killed. The federal government sent in the army to suppress what it considered to be a rebellion. Spurred on by the success of Riel's forces against the Mounties, angry Natives on the plains joined the resistance to foreign rule.

Based on his opening comments in the next chapter, Henry Ross Halpin did not understand many of the realities of the Plains Cree. For most of his life he had been in the northern parts of what became Manitoba, Saskatchewan, and Alberta, living among the Woods Cree and Swampy Cree whose culture and diet were considerably different from that of the Plains Cree who lived on the plains. After reserves had been established by the numbered treaties, the Plains Cree and other tribes were restricted to those stipulated areas. Their staple food supply had been the bison, which did not respect reserve boundaries, roaming the whole of the central plains that extended through the continent of North America. After the introduction of the repeating rifle, bison numbers were decimated. Greedy American Buffalo hunters had even set grass fires to prevent the bison from migrating back into Canada. The Plains Cree and Blackfoot in the southern part of what would become Alberta and Saskatchewan began to starve. Their pleas for help were often ignored, leading to confrontations with Indian agents and the police. Halpin had not seen what had happened to them after the southern treaties were signed because he was working in the Far North.

Fed up with his situation, Big Bear had moved his band from the southern plains to the parkland region near Frog Lake where there were other sources of food that they could hunt and trap. Again a conflict arose with the local Indian agent Thomas Quinn over where Big Bear's people were to settle. When Big Bear seemed powerless to arrange a satisfactory location for his people, his tribal authority was challenged by younger men in his band. When news of Riel's victory over the police at Duck Lake reached them, they were spurred on in their resistance to white rule. Fuelled by ongoing conflicts with Thomas Quinn, and by alcohol, their anger exploded, leading to the murder of the Indian agent, six whites who were working with him, and two Catholic missionaries.

In the next chapter, we pick up Halpin's own story of his involvement in these events from his shorter memoir.

12 A Prisoner with Big Bear[1]

*A*ll through the fall and winter of 1884 and 1885 there had been general talk of trouble to come between the Indians and Halfbreeds and the government of the North-West Territories, but no faith was placed in these rumours, nor do I think any trouble was taken by anyone to find out if there was any mischief brewing or what the grievances of the Indians and both the English-speaking and French-speaking Métis were. I, for my part, heard declarations over and over again that there was going to be a *quart d'heure* [a piece of action] in the spring, but having lived so long with Native people and knowing that they were well off and looked after, I put no faith in the stories. Nor do I in this sketch intend to cover the ground that is said to have led up to the little trouble that occurred in the spring of 1885. I only wish to give a plain unvarnished story of my own life during the two months I was a prisoner with Chief Big Bear and his gang of renegade warriors.

I took charge of the Hudson's Bay Company post at Cold Lake [now in Alberta] in the early winter of 1884 and 1885 for the purpose of trading with the Natives of that district. The winter was a hard one and very little fur was taken. The Indians of Cold Lake are mostly Chipewyan and are a thrifty lot of people — good hunters and have or had at that time, a good herd of cattle about them.

I was going back from Frog Lake to my post at Cold Lake [on the 19th of March] and I met Big Bear camped there on the road.... I told him

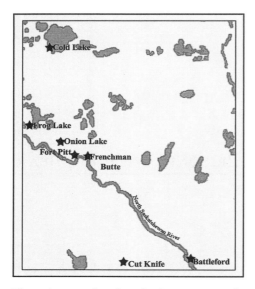

Places Associated with Halpin's Experience of the Northwest Rebellion, 1885.

I had seen in the *Battleford Herald*, and [heard] at Frog Lake, that there was trouble in Batôche, and that Riel had stopped the mails there. I told him I thought there was likely to be trouble. His reply was, "I think it very strange." His reply was in Cree. He was surprised to hear about it....

I stopped and had dinner with him.... I invited him to come up to my house at Cold Lake, come out and see me there, and he came.... He came to my house before dinner on the 21st and went away on the evening of the 22nd.... He wanted to go home and hunt; he mentioned that to me during the evening, and at three o'clock, before a heavy wind, he said he thought he would start home this evening and go around in the bush, and he might get a chance, it was blowing so hard, to kill a moose in the bush....[2]

On the evening of the 3rd of April 1885, I had just come home after an afternoon of unsuccessful hunting, tired out from tramping through the slush and water along the lakes where I had been looking for an early duck or anything else that turned up. I was sitting outside my house waiting for the Native boy I had as a servant to get supper ready and wishing for anything, no matter what, to change the loneliness of my present position.

I had been expecting for some days past a gang of men from Frog Lake who were coming out to me to saw lumber for flat boats, which were to be used in the freighting of a quantity of flour (then at Cold Lake in my charge) down the Beaver River to Île-à-la-Crosse for the Hudson's Bay Company[3] and was beginning to wonder at the delay, as the river was opening in many places and should in a short time be navigable.

All at once I heard voices, and looking up saw five or six mounted Indians coming towards the house. I turned to my boy who was busy with the supper and told him he would have to get more as the men we were expecting had arrived. He acted rather strange I thought, so I asked him what he thought they were after, and he used an Indian word that means "they are on the war path."

When they came a little closer I began to think that something was wrong for I saw that at least three of them were mounted on North West Mounted Police horses from Frog Lake. They stopped a short distance from where I was sitting and I got up and went forward to them when they all dismounted. They shook hands with me and seemed in a good humour, laughing and joking with each other and with my servant and me.

I said I was glad to see them and asked them if they had come to build the flat boats. Lone Man, a son-in-law of Big Bear, who seemed to be in charge of the lot, acted as speaker and told me that they had only come to visit me and not to work. One of the Indians, who had worked with Mr. Simpson of the Hudson's Bay Company at Frog Lake, then took my boy aside and had some talk with him. They came back to me in a few minutes, and I could see by my boy's face that he had heard something to startle him, for he was as pale as possible for an Native to get and trembling with excitement.

He then went out and I followed him, asking him what was the matter. He said I would soon find out, and took my gun from where it was hanging and started to put on his coat and prepare himself as if he were going out. I told him to hurry and get supper as the men must be hungry after their ride. He did not answer but started out the door saying he was going after the horses. I told him I did not want the horses, but he went off down the road and paid no attention to me. By this time I was getting angry and started after him with my mind made up to give him a pounding. I caught up with him, seized him by the collar of his coat, and took the gun from him. He told me to take care or I might get into trouble.

Just then Lone Man came up and told me to let the boy go for the horses and that he had something to tell me in the house. When I began to think a little I decided it was best to do what he wanted, so I went back with him. Back in the house I found the other Indians drinking tea seasoned with pain killer which they had taken out of the store. I told them they had no business to touch anything in the house without asking me as I was in charge of it. Then they all got up and shook hands with me, one after another. This I knew from experience was the beginning of a long talk of some kind. After the handshaking they all sat down but Lone Man, who began to speak. He said to me, "You have always been a good friend of mine, and also of the others [of] our friends since you came here last fall. We all like you but we want you to tell us what you would do in case there was any trouble with the white people and the Police. Which side would you take? We would like to know now, before we return to Frog Lake?"

At this moment one of the other Cree men got up and asked me what I thought of Louis Riel and would I help him if he were fighting with the police. Happening just then to look round, I saw two of them changing their own blanket coats for coats out of the store (which was in my house). I stood up and told them to take them off. But they said no, that everything in the country now belonged to them, at the same time handing me a note written on a small scrap of paper out of a pocket book.

The note was from William B. Cameron of Frog Lake and ran, as nearly as I can remember now, as follows: "Dear Halpin, the Crees are going out to see you. They have killed all the white people here.[4] Don't offer any opposition to them. They say they will not hurt you."

You may be sure I was, as the saying is, "knocked all of a heap" and felt that I would have to be very careful what I said to them. They could see that I felt very much the news contained in the note, but they all again shook hands and told me I was quite safe so long as I did what they told me, and promised not to try and get away from them. If I did try to escape they said they would shoot me. Besides there was no place I could go as all the white people in the country, or so I thought, had been killed by this time. They then told me about the fight at Duck Lake with the police and volunteers from Prince Albert, and, of course, made it appear the victory was in their favour. After this I made up my mind to take things easy and make-believe to concur with all they said and did, but the horror of that night will never be forgotten by me should I live a thousand years.

Horse Child, son of Big Bear, and W.B. Cameron of the Hudson's Bay Company, 1885.

My man got back with the horses by this time and after he had put them in the stable, he came into the house. I then told him to make some bread for the Indians who had up to this time had nothing to eat. He turned round to me and said, "I have been working long enough, so you must do the cooking now." He looked very ugly. How I wish I had him somewhere I could give him a couple of good Irish blows to the face and bring him to his senses! For even then, with everything in his favour, I could see the little brute tremble at his own audacity. Anyway, I set to work and set out their supper and made up my mind that if any chance came, I would run off that night, trusting to luck to find my way, and strike out down Beaver River for Île-á-la-Crosse, warning the priest at the mission about seven miles from where I then was. I would tell him of what had occurred and give him a chance to join me.

After the supper was over they all sat down and smoked, chatting as if nothing but the most friendly feeling existed between us. It was now quite dark and I had in the meantime, when I thought they were not watching, picked up several boxes of matches and a small ball of twine and some snaring wire and secreted them about my person, for I had fully made up my mind to run for it. But I found it was not so easy to get away, for whenever I went to the door or tried to go outside for anything, my servant boy would follow me with the gun and wait until I sat down again. Oh, how I hated that little brute that night, and do so still! I don't think I could ever think him anything but a most contemptible hound, for I had been most kind to him in every way and made much of him. So, burning with indignation at him, and my heart almost bursting with grief at the calamity that had occurred at Frog Lake, I lay down on my bed and pretended to sleep, but sleep was far from me that night and for many a night after.

The Cree had lain down on the floor, one of them staying awake all the time, so I had no chance to get out of the house. A little after midnight they all got up and took all the goods belonging to the store and divided the objects equally among the six of them. After they put the stuff in bales or bundles handy to carry on horseback, they told me to put on my clothes as we were going down to the mission to kill the priest there and to go through the store of the trader who lived near the mission.

I made myself ready as soon as possible, having an idea that I could get away from my captors on the road. Again I found that I was mistaken and that they meant to take good care of me. They took an old cart that stood near the house and hitched a horse to it, telling me to get in. They then tied me securely so that all chance of escape was cut off. The night was very cold and the roads very bad. In my cramped position, with my arms fastened to each side of the cart, I was soon half-frozen and splashed all over with mud and water off the cart wheels. We had travelled some distance towards the mission, when they stopped at the house of one of the local Chipewyan and told them what had happened at Frog Lake.

I told the Chipewyan that I thought the Cree had made up their mind to kill the priest, Father Le Goff. However, before this, they had coolly offered me the position of executioner of the above-named priest, which I could not see my way to accept. Seemingly, they thought it rather strange that I did not jump at such an offer.[5]

The Chipewyan did not appear to like the business very much, especially the killing of the two priests [at Frog Lake], and from what little of their language I could understand, I soon made up my mind that if any idea of killing Father Le Goff was still in the minds of Big Bear's Cree, they had better be very careful, as I was quite sure the Chipewyan would kill the whole lot of them before they let them touch their priest.

I was very much pleased to see this, as I was afraid till then that the poor priest was going to be butchered like the people at Frog Lake — in cold blood. After waiting about an hour we started once more towards the mission, some Chipewyan having joined us. There must have been about ten or twelve mounted Native men altogether.

I again felt cold and asked Lone Man to let me get out of the cart and run to keep warm. He was quite willing, but my boy was against it, but Lone Man let me out, telling me not to try any tricks as I was sure to come to grief if I did. Of course by this time I saw that there was very little use in trying to get away from them that night, so I went along quietly.

When we arrived at the mission we went into the priest's house and found him still in bed. I told him what had happened and I think he thought his hour was come. He was very much affected, poor fellow, but not on his own account, but more so for the murder of his fellow missionaries at Frog Lake. The Chipewyan took him out of harm's way at once for they were afraid to leave him with the Cree. The river ran close to the mission, and, while the priest and I were walking up and down outside the church, I asked him to risk it and try and get away. But he said no. His place was with his people when they were in trouble, and besides he would go to Frog Lake and bury the priests who had been murdered there. When I saw that he had made up his mind to stay with his people and not risk getting off, I thought it best to wait for some better chance myself, trying to keep in with the Cree as best I could.

After Big Bear's men had gone through the priest's house and church, they started for the trader's house about a mile away. He was up and it seemed to me at the time that he did not appear very much surprised at what the Natives told him. The women of the house set to work and soon had a good breakfast ready for the party after which the Cree told the trader to go to his store and take anything he wanted for his family and himself in the way of clothing and provisions, for they would take the balance for themselves. He helped himself to what he wanted and told me to help myself. I took a pocket knife and some tobacco, more to make it appear that I was in with them, than that I wanted anything gained in such a way.

Again the Indians divided the goods amongst themselves and made ready to return to Frog Lake, first making the Chipewyan promise to get ready and come after them in a day or so. The Cree were very anxious to have the Chipewyan with them at Frog Lake as they, the Chips, had a very fine band of cattle, which would be a good thing when other kinds of provisions were in short supply. I thought at the time that starvation would soon come. The Indians, if wanting an empty sack for any purpose would take a bag of flour and empty it outside the door. Hundreds of bags of flour were destroyed in this way, both at Cold Lake and other places where there was any flour stored.

The party in charge now started on the return journey to Frog Lake, putting me on an old horse that could hardly walk and making me go ahead of them on the road. They were all very lively, talking, laughing, and making jokes about the way the people had been killed at Frog Lake. Of course this interested me very much, and I kept thinking how I would look carried around on hay forks by a band of howling warriors, this last mentioned performance they told the Chipewyan, had been enacted at Frog Lake a day or so before. They seemed to think it very good fun.

Imasees or Little Bear, son of Big Bear. It was Little Bear who instigated the murders at Frog Lake in 1885.

In going about camp I had to be very careful what I said or did as I found all the Natives very quick to take offence, in fact "spoiling for a row" with anyone that wanted to have one. The first evening I was in camp I came very close to getting into trouble while trying to prevent two Indian boys who were both armed with guns, from killing each other. I don't know what the trouble was about, but there was a lot of loud talk and suddenly one of them put his gun to the other's breast and pulled the trigger. The gun was one of the old-fashioned flintlocks and luckily did not go off or the youngster would have been dead. I tried to stop them, but it was no use, and I started for the tent of Wandering Spirit who was the "War Chief" and boss of the camp. I told him that if he did not want the boys to kill each other he had better have them parted. He came and spoke to them and they parted, but Wandering Spirit told me [...] to mind my own affairs. I concluded it was best to do this and not to say a word to prevent any little festivities that they might wish to engage in in the future.

That night Lone Man gave me a part of his tent for my own and told me to make myself at home and that I was all right now, as Big Bear wanted to treat the Hudson's Bay Company's people well. I must say I did not feel much at home with one of Lone Man's children at each side of me, put there, he said, to keep me from harm, but I knew he meant to keep me from trying to run away during the night.

I do not think I closed my eyes that first night. There was a constant hubbub all over the camp. Scouts would arrive and then the camp was all excitement to hear the latest news. When anyone passed close to the tent where I lay I felt quite sure he was going to fire through the tent and kill me. The only wish I had was that he would make his shot a sure one and finish me at once. I did not want to be wounded and suffer for a long time before I died. But I slept through the night at last. I don't think I was ever so glad in my life before to see dawn, but during the whole time I was in that camp I never felt quite safe.

Next morning, the 6th of April, I think, I took a walk around the camp to see my fellow prisoners, Mrs. Delaney and Mrs. Gowanlock, who were under the charge of John Pritchard, the government interpreter at Frog Lake. How I pitied these two poor women! Mrs. Delaney seemed to bear up better as far as one could judge by outward signs, but one could see by her face what she was suffering. Mrs. Gowanlock was only a shadow of the handsome girl I had seen at Battleford a few months before, and I would not have known her. She was completely prostrated with grief and when she tried to speak, she would burst into tears.

At that time I thought it would have been better for both those women if they had died with their husbands and I recalled the horrible stories I had read of the Indians' treatment of their female prisoners, but let me say that here once and for all, that I do not think that once during their stay in camp that either of those women was molested in any way. Of course, they had many influential Métis on their side, which tended to keep the young men in their place. These two women had to work for the Natives, sewing, making bread, and things of that kind, and, most of the time, had to work from morning to night, which I think was good for both of them. Had they had been left alone with their own sad thoughts they might have died. All the Métis prisoners did their best to appear at home, but, on the whole, I think the Indians distrusted them more than they did the white prisoners.

The camp was pitched on a high hill overlooking Frog Lake and was in a very good position in case of surprise attack. Of course, if any considerable number of men had caught them in that place, they would have been driven into the lake. The camp was well-decorated; nearly all the tents had a flag of some kind or another and their medicine bags were all decked with ribbons and hanging on poles near the tents. Both the Native men and their wives were dressed in all the finery they could get and there were some very unusual costumes.

After I had been for a few days in camp I was free to go anywhere within bounds, so I had a very good opportunity of seeing all that was going on. There was one thing that struck me very soon, and that was the changed bearing of the Native women towards their husbands. I asked Lone Man's wife the reason for it. She told me that as there was no law now, the Indian could murder or beat his wife to his heart's content without fear of the police. At other times, such was not the case, as when a Native man did anything of that sort the law would arrest him.

As a general thing, Native women rule their husbands, and as long as they don't go too far, the men seem to take it in good part. But at times the women get a "big head" and their husbands can stand them no longer and beat them. If things get too bad the women call in help of the police or

Indian Department officials. But when in this camp with Big Bear I don't think I ever saw such a submissive lot of women in my life. Lone Man's wife had a tongue in her head before the trouble began that no one could stand better than her husband. She ruled him with a rod of iron, but now she had not a word to say and Lone Man "made hay while the sun shone." He used to come home from some council or dog feast and try and pick a quarrel with his wife, whether she wanted to or not. I have seen him take a stick of firewood and hit her over the back for no reason, other than to show her that he was boss of the shanty. There was no use saying anything, and after the shindig was over, they were or appeared to be good friends.

The little Indian boys also became very "big-spoken and saucy" to their mothers, taking the pattern of their fathers, they now looked down on females. Their mothers and the other women dared not so much as lift a hand to them. Even in times of peace a mother seldom if ever hits one of her sons, though she has full swing at her daughters, so long as they live at home, whether grown up or not.

The Indians, although they used me very well, so far as giving me plenty to eat and drink went, managed to make me feel at all times that the white people in the camp were only there on probation. Any show of temper or any attempt to get away would be met with death, and they told us as much, for they were afraid we would give information as to their whereabouts and fighting strength. But on these first days of our imprisonment it was more than just impossible to escape. All of us were closely watched on all sides, even when we did not think we were.

Lone Man, my host for the time, often used to ask me what I thought the future would bring for the Native people after the way in which they had acted. After I had expressed my thought of what the ultimate end of the trouble would be, he would laugh and say "perhaps [you are] right," but that Riel was a very clever man, almost a god in fact, and could make no mistake as to the outcome of the rebellion, and that Riel had told Big Bear the previous fall that all the Indians and Halfbreeds were going to be rich beyond even their expectations, after they had driven the whites out of the country. He also said that the buffalo would come back to the plains again and there would be unlimited food once more without much work. Food without work was their idea of happiness.

I visited Mrs. Gowanlock and Mrs. Delaney every day and saw how they were getting along. They at all times seemed to be employed at some work for their captors. I don't think they had many idle moments in those days. [...] But it was well for those women that the Métis purchased them from their captors [for several horses and some money], or I am quite sure the debt of vengeance owed by the whites for those days of trouble would be much heavier. The Halfbreeds in the camp acted splendidly and nothing but praise can be given to Pritchard, Blondin, Beaudreau, and others, who at much personal risk, saved those poor women from a life that could have been a hundred times worse than death.[8]

After we had been in camp a week or so I think we were not watched so closely and we had greater freedom in going about the camp. We seemed to be welcome into whatever tent we entered and the best of food that was in the tent was placed before us. We were treated as if things were as before the trouble began. Still the Indians and Halfbreeds showed plainly that they knew they were masters of the situation. Natives are like Irish people, naturally hospitable, always giving the best the house can afford to the guests. There were many times I went back to my tent uncomfortably feasted, for it did not do to refuse to eat.

Some of the dishes set before one in the camp I do not think would be very tempting to some Regina people. I have seen beef, bacon, gophers, fish, dried apples, raisins, potatoes with the skin on, and many other articles boiled in the same pot at the same time. So I leave it to your imagination what the taste of the mess would be. To me it seemed that the fish came out on top.

Some of the costumes were also amusing in the extreme, for whenever there was a feast or council going on, every man, woman, and child in camp, who attended, tried to have some sort of finery in the way or painted faces or loudly coloured clothing to show off. I remember one, named Dressy Man, going about dressed in the following outfit. To begin with his feet, he wore one police boot and one moccasin. On his legs were a pair of police riding pants. His coat was an evening swallow tail, which he wore back to front and on which he had sewn many rows of brass buttons and little strings of coloured beads. To crown it all, he wore a police helmet painted red on one side and green on the other, and from the spike, […] hung a pair of ladies' velvet slippers, one on each side of his head. All of this finery, combined with a painted face, made Dressy Man the most envied man in camp.

Native women are very fond of bright and glaring combinations of colours in their clothing. Green, red, and yellow are the prime favourites, and when all these colours are combined in one dress, they are happy for the time being. But like their white sisters, they get unhappy when they see another who has, to their mind, a nicer dress than they have, and, as their white sisters are supposed to do, they make remarks that are not always complimentary. I have seen a woman come to visit another simply to show off a new dress with all the colours of the rainbow in it. And though the dress was admired and the different points in its makeup praised to the face of the owner, and though the women would kiss one another when parting, and act very much like their white sisters at such time, I have heard them, after their visitor had departed, express their opinion that the dress was a failure and their friend was a fright. Indian women never wear hats or bonnets; at least they did not in that camp or there might have been more trouble.

After we had been there a week or more, the Chipewyan arrived from Cold Lake to join Big Bear's men. This, I think, added about 150 or two hundred souls to the camp. And, as they brought a good many of their cattle with them, they were gladly received by the Cree. Had they come empty-handed, the welcome would not have been so great. Big Bear's men had by this time killed nearly all the cattle on the reserve for beef. I have seen them kill four or five animals at one time just for the fun or pleasure of taking life and even the little boys would take their fathers' gun and go out and shoot a calf or cow so as to appear big before the other boys in the camp.

After the Chipewyan arrived with their priest Father Le Goff, efforts were made to bury the people who were killed on the 3rd of April. So a party of us went down to where the massacre had taken place. Most of the bodies were lying just where they had been shot, and as the weather had been cold, no change had taken place in their appearance. […] Indian agent Thomas Quinn and his interpreter Charles Gouin had been thrown into a cellar after having been stripped. Then a plentiful amount of coal oil had been poured over them and the house set on fire.

Courtesy of the Glenbow Archives, NA-3409-20

Photo of a group at Fort Pitt in 1884 (from left to right): Thomas Quinn, Indian agent, murdered at Frog Lake, 1885; Inspector Francis J. Dickens, NWMP (son of novelist Charles Dickens); James Keith Simpson, HBC clerk, Fort Pitt; Frederick Stanley Simpson; and Angus McKay, HBC.

The Indian agent, who was much hated by all the Natives, was mutilated to a degree. They seemed not to be able to show enough hatred to him, even after he was dead. Whether or not he merited this hatred is not for me to say now, but after they got through with him, I don't think his own mother would have known him. Even Quinn's wife, who was related to Big Bear and many of his people, never raised her hand or voice to save her husband. Had she even done so, I am not sure if she could have saved him on that dreadful day, the 3rd of April, Good Friday, I think it was.

There were nine people killed on that morning, namely Indian Agent Quinn; Charles Gouin, carpenter and interpreter; John Delaney, farming instructor; J.A. Gowanlock; William Gilchrist; and John Williscraft who were building a mill for the Natives at the time at Frog Lake. Also killed were John Dill, a trader, and two priests.

There is a gap in the manuscript at this point. It resumes after a message had arrived from Louis Riel asking Big Bear's tribe to join his rebellion.

All this good news tended to raise the spirits of the Cree and make them more saucy and proud, and though I felt at the time that most of the stories were false, I could not say so without laying myself under their displeasure, as they trusted their runners and their letters without question. From this time forward I don't think we were allowed as much freedom in the camp or were treated as well. There were so many people in the camp who had lost friends and relations in the fight with the police and Prince Albert Volunteers[9] at the fight at Duck Lake in March, and they now heard of it for the first time. This, of course. tended to make them cranky and morose, but no one showed any open hostility to any of the white people in the camp, but still they were not treated the same as before in many ways.

After the Chipewyan came to the camp and had rested their horses and themselves for a few days, preparations were made for a trip to Fort Pitt where the Mounted Police still held out in the Hudson's Bay Company fort. Since the Company had a good stock of goods on hand, the Natives were anxious to take the place, without fighting if they could do so, but take it they would, at all risks.

I heard Big Bear demur against going there one day; he did not want to go.... He wanted to go another direction altogether; he did not want to go towards Battleford, but wanted to pitch out to Turtle or Moose Lake instead.... I know he tried to get them not to go.[10]

So after orders had been given to the old men who were left behind to keep up almost hourly communication [by way of using smoke signals] with the fighting men who were on the way to Fort Pitt, about 150 to 200 mounted Natives started for Onion Lake en route to the Fort. I think it was on Monday the 13th of April that we started. The day was fine and warm and the snow had almost all gone, only in places was a little left, though the ice on Frog Lake was still quite strong and firm. Some wagons and carts were taken along to carry back the spoils of the campaign, for they were quite confident about the result of the trip and never for a moment thought the police would stand them off. Where they got this confidence from I don't know, for whenever the police and the Indians had come to face each other in the past, the police always came off best, even when the Native force had ten to one in their favour. Riel's victory at Duck Lake showed that the police were not invincible. But this fear of the police was all over for the time being, not that I think they would have stood up and fought with half the number of police on anything like fair grounds, for they are naturally cowardly in the daytime, or when the odds are not considerably in their favour.

I was about the last to start out of the camp.... I was driving a cart for Lone Man.... I saw Big Bear; he was away at the back of the caravan, and I too was about as far back as I could get, and he was there.... I was told I had better go forward [to the front of the group]. Big Bear said if there were any letters or anything to be written to the people in the fort, I who understood the Cree language and that sort of thing, would be able to understand what they said and write letters for them.... He thought if I went down there and wrote letters, and that sort of thing, I might be able to get the people to come out of the fort peacefully and prevent any bloodshed that might have been committed there.[11]

When we got to Onion Lake,[12] we found all the buildings deserted and one or two had been burned. The Natives started to destroy everything that had been left in the storehouses and dwelling houses. Flour and bacon were plentiful and the Indians ate all they wanted and tried to waste the remainder. Flour was emptied out on the dirty ground by the sackful and trampled under foot. Sides of good bacon were thrown out in the mud and fed to the dogs or in other ways destroyed — anything to spoil what was needed.

We had not seen anyone on the road from Frog Lake to Onion Lake, but some scouts belonging to the camp said that they had spotted some Mounted Police later in the day some distance from the road. We put in the night at Onion Lake, the Indians feasting and dancing. Early in the morning we started for the fort, with the Natives dancing and singing along the road, and now and then firing off a gun to keep everyone on the alert. When we reached a spot about five miles from the fort, Big Bear came to me and asked me to write a letter to Captain Dickens,[13] who was in charge of the police of Fort Pitt, asking him to give up the fort and take the police with him. If he would go without fighting, he could do so, but that if he would not go out, he would have to fight and that Big Bear would kill everyone in the fort or burn them out like rats in a hole.

An old Hudson's Bay Company servant delivered the letter, and Dickens sent back word for the Indians to come on, that he was ready for them, and would not give up the fort so long as a man remained alive. This brought the situation before Big Bear and his party into a different light and they began to realize that if they wanted to be proprietors of Fort Pitt they were going to have some work to do first. It made them angry to think that the police in Fort Pitt would not vacate the place as did the police at Frog Lake the night before the Indians killed the whites there.[14] There was much loud talk from a lot of the young men of what they would do, and in an hour or so while we were resting, they got themselves worked up into a very bad state of mind.

I felt that very much depended on the next day or so, as to whether any of the white prisoners in the camp at Frog Lake would ever get out of it alive for I heard some of the Indians say that for each one of them killed in the taking of Fort Pitt one of the white people would die. This was not pleasant news and I at once tried all in my power to get them in a better frame of mind. I told them I would do all possible to see the Hudson's Bay people in the fort and get things settled quietly. The Natives at that time only wanted the goods that were in the fort, and also, if possible, that the police would go leave without fighting.

It was late in the afternoon before we made a start on the last stage of our journey to Fort Pitt and it was almost sunset before we arrived at the top of the hill overlooking the Saskatchewan River, on the banks of which the fort was situated. When we came within sight of the fort we could see that the inmates were quite prepared for us. Everything that an Indian could use as ambush had been cleared away from around the place and the gates closed, and the place looked to be shipshape. High above all floated the dear old Union Jack.

I don't ever remember looking upon that flag before with so much love as I did that day, and would have given a good deal to be with its defenders inside the fort. But I could not get a chance to get down, though I asked the Cree to let me go and see Captain Francis Dickens and Mr.

William McLean who was the Hudson's Bay agent in Fort Pitt [and Halpin's immediate superior] and make some sort of bargain with them, but instead they sent an old man by the name of Dufresne [a Hudson's Bay Company employee, listed in the 1881 census as being French with a Native wife], to speak to the people in the fort.

There was a problem of authority at Fort Pitt, which was a Hudson's Bay Company fort with William McLean in charge. Dickens and his Mounties had retreated to the fort for their own protection. Dickens was an officer whose name outshone his abilities. It is evident that McLean was not taking orders from the Mounties and he was far more experienced in dealing with the Cree than was Dickens. On April 14, McLean, trying to negotiate with the Cree, left the fort and entered the Indian camp, and established a temporary truce to stop the attack on Fort Pitt. McLean then returned to the fort.

Later that day Big Bear dictated another letter to Halpin to be sent to Sergeant J.A. Martin of the North West Mounted Police at Fort Pitt. It read:

My dear friend: Since I have met you long ago we have always been good friends, and you have from time to time given me things. This is the reason why I want to speak kindly to you, so please try to get off from Fort Pitt as soon as you can, and tell your captain that I remember him well. For since the Canadian Government have had me to starve in this county, he sometimes gave me food. I do not forget the last time I visited Pitt, he gave me a good blanket; this is the reason that I want you all out without any bloodshed; we had a talk, I and my men, before we left camp, and we thought the way we are doing now the best. This is to let you off, if you would go, so try and get away before the afternoon, as the young men are all wild and hard to keep in hand. P.S. You asked me to keep the men in camp last night and I did so, so I want you to get off to-day."[15]

This letter is significant as it demonstrates that Big Bear was indeed trying to avert the attack and save lives, but he was having difficulty controlling the young men, including his own sons. The letter was published that year in Charles Pelham Mulvaney's The History of the North-West Rebellion.

Nothing was done that night for all the Natives were tired after their trip from Frog Lake. So eating, drinking, and big talk was the order of the day or rather night. Early in the morning the camp was all astir, with scouts arriving from Frog Lake and other parts of the country. Others from the camp started off for Battleford, Saddle Lake, and Duck Lake. Many of the Métis left us while at Pitt, also heading for Battleford and Duck Lake, and never came back again.

Smoke signals were to be seen in many directions during the day. The Indians know quite well what each particular "smoke" means. They have some way of holding blankets over the fire and shaking them in a particular fashion so as to make the smoke come up at different intervals and directions, each of which has a meaning. We in the camp at Frog Lake, more than a hundred miles from Cut Knife, knew all about the battle[16] that took place there on the same afternoon it occurred simply through the use of Indian signals.

Halpin's shorter memoir ends at this point. The rest of his story has been recreated from an 1894 newspaper report of one of his speeches and also from his testimony at the Rebellion Trials. Commentary has also been added to explain gaps in his account.

On the 15th of April, Hudson's Bay Company official McLean, again trying to negotiate with the renegade Cree, left the fort by himself and went to their camp. Things were going well until three Mounties were spotted nearby. Dickens had sent police scouts out from the fort to spy on the Natives several days before and as they were returning to Fort Pitt, they stumbled upon the Cree camp. Thinking they were under attack, the Cree opened fire on the policemen. One never made it back to the fort, but was killed on top of a bank about a quarter of a mile away from safety. Halpin was an eyewitness to his murder.

I was in the thick of the fight at Fort Pitt and I saw Corporal Cowan shot and fall from his horse, and be mutilated by "Dressy Man" and others. Also Constable Loasby was also shot in two places by Lone Man, Big Bear's son-in-law. But Loasby managed to get into the fort and I am glad to say that he is still alive today.[17]

After this battle, McLean was taken prisoner by the young Native men. Within the fort confusion reigned. Captain Dickens, who had earned a reputation in Canada for incompetence and alcoholism, had no control over the occupants of the fort. The remaining civilians, including McLean's family, left the fort and surrendered to the Cree, who took them prisoner.

The police left the fort the night of the fight in a flat-boat and after a safe trip reached Battleford.

The rebel Cree then looted Fort Pitt. Halpin and Big Bear, who had opposed the looting, watched from the hill overlooking the fort. Later they went down to survey the damage. Armed with their loot and the additional prisoners, the Cree headed back to Frog Lake.

After our return to Frog Lake, the Cree spent time in feasting, war dancing, dog feasts, etc. . . . . There was a murder of an old woman; the main cause was the Indians' superstitious dread of an insane person. She, for some days before, had been prophesying events unfavourable to the Native people. They wanted Mr. McLean to kill her, as they thought they could not do it themselves, but he declined the honour, so a Métis named Charlebois took the matter in hand, covered her with a shawl and crushed her head with a hickory stick, after which they chopped her head into small pieces and burnt it while the others were making grand preparations for a "sun dance."[18]

On or about the 5th of May, the Cree returned with their prisoners to Fort Pitt. After that they wandered the countryside seeking to avoid the police and the army. They arrived at Frenchman Butte, about twenty miles east of Fort Pitt on or about the 27th of May.

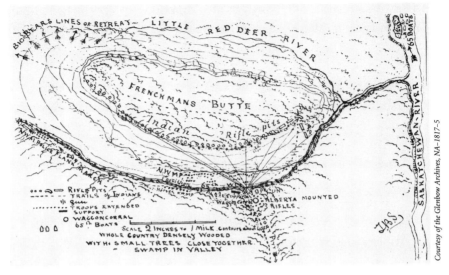

Map of Battle of Frenchman Butte, May 1885.

At Frenchman Butte news came of the arrival of the troops at Fort Pitt, which put a stop to the proceedings and all left in a hurry for Red Deer Creek, where the fight with the troops under Major-General [Thomas Bland] Strange[19] took place on the 28th of May.

Here, the Cree put me to making rifle pits, and gave me a butcher knife and frying pan with which to dig. I managed with these things to make a hole about seven feet long, four feet deep, and three feet broad after a hard day's work. After this, in the evening, I did some marvellous work loading shells for some of them, and I think the shells were more dangerous to the person behind the gun than to one in front of it. Some of these shells were all powder mixed with caps; in others there was nothing but shot.

For about two hours next morning during the fight I was kept tied to a tree by a Native named Ka-we-che-twa-mat. During the thick of the fight several shells thrown into the camp came too near me to be comfortable. A Cree, whom I knew well, let me loose from my uncomfortable position, and I made my escape back into the woods. Since previous to this my clothing had been appropriated, I resembled an Indian too closely to show myself to the troops. After several days of wandering through the

156

bush I fell in with Dr. J.P. Pennyfather, the military surgeon and some scouts who treated me most kindly and took me to their camp."[20]

Once he had regained his freedom, after sixty-two days of captivity and terror, Henry Halpin, along with W.B. Cameron, his fellow fur trader and prisoner, joined Major-General Strange's Alberta Field Force. Halpin and Cameron used their vast knowledge of the area, working as scouts and guides, as the hunt was on to bring to justice those who had perpetrated the Frog Lake Massacre, the looting and burning of Fort Pitt, the murder of Corporal Cowan, and the other crimes associated with those events.

As the search progressed, the government and the newspapers portrayed Big Bear as the arch-villain, even though he had nothing to do with the crimes, but his first letter to Dickens, which had more to do with posturing in front of his own people to avoid bloodshed than being a real threat, had implicated him in the murders. Halpin next saw Big Bear in the cells at Prince Albert after he turned himself in near Carlton House.[21]

With the ordeal behind him, Halpin took a holiday and visited his brother Nicholas, who was a pharmacist in Brandon, Manitoba. He did some public speaking about his experiences as a prisoner. The reporter for the Brandon Weekly Mail *exaggerated his terror by saying that Halpin was often scalped while he was a prisoner.[22]*

During the Rebellion trials, which followed in August 1885, Henry Halpin testified for the defence of Big Bear, saying that his friend Big Bear was just as much a victim of the circumstances as he [Halpin] was. He stated that fellow captive and Hudson's Bay Company employee Stanley Simpson said he thought "it was strange, very strange, that any white man [Halpin] should get on the defence of an Indian. His idea was that the Indians should be hanged."[23]

Halpin attributed his safety to his friendship with Big Bear and the general respect that Natives had for the Hudson's Bay Company.[24] All the white captives, except Stanley Simpson, testified that Big Bear was innocent and powerless to stop the young men in his band from committing the murders, seizing Fort Pitt, and engaging in battle with the troops at Frenchman Butte.[25] If anything, Big Bear's influence had averted further bloodshed. In spite of the clear testimony of Big Bear's innocence, the judge's

Courtesy of the Glenbow Archives, NA-1270-1

Big Bear as a prisoner, 1885.

prejudicial statements swayed the jury, which found him guilty of treason-felony, but with a recommendation for mercy. They had only deliberated for fifteen minutes! Stipendiary Magistrate Hugh Richardson sentenced Big Bear to three years in Stony Mountain Penitentiary.[26]

Big Bear served less than two years in prison before he was released. He was a sick old man and the government did not want him dying in prison. He lived less than a year after being let out.

Some of the Natives who had been involved in the Frog Lake Massacre and the killing of Constable Cowan at Fort Pitt were also caught and tried, and Halpin testified against them. Six of them and two other Cree were executed in a mass hanging at Fort Battleford.

The payment Henry Ross Halpin received for searching for rebel Cree.

Those men who had served the government in hunting down the Cree renegades were awarded compensation by the government. When Halpin applied for his wages for his time with the Alberta Field Force, he was turned down. The War Claims Commission ruled: "This man appears to have been one of the prisoners whom the troops were sent to release. He ought to be thankful instead of making such a claim."[27] *The following year he re-applied for compensation for his services; he eventually received the standard $80 compensation.*[28]

13 Muscowpetung, Fort Pelly, and Indian Affairs

*A*s a result of Halpin's ordeal and his prominent role in the Rebellion trials, he attracted the attention of the Indian Affairs Department and an approach was made to hire him. No doubt its officials were impressed by his extensive knowledge of the Cree people and their language. To avert more Native rebellions the Canadian government sought to appoint as Indian agents those men who had some empathy for the Native Peoples. "Bay" men had a fairly good history in their dealings with Natives, at least a lot better than some of the central Canadian urban bureaucrats who had obtained their jobs primarily through political patronage appointments. The job offer from Indian Affairs could not have come at a better time. Halpin needed work, by now he was thirty-one years old. When he had reached Prince Albert after escaping from the renegade Cree, he was told that his services with the Hudson's Bay Company were no longer required and he was dismissed.[1] He had anticipated that the Company might renew his contract or even promote him because of his courage during the Rebellion.

Halpin wrote to Joseph Wrigley, the new commissioner of the Hudson's Bay Company, outlining his past experience with the Company, explaining his past failures and successes, supplying a list of references from HBC men at Fort Qu'Appelle, Edmonton, Peace River, and his last employer Mr. McLean, and pleading for another posting:

Now Sir, I think it rather hard after nearly ten years service to give up the trade and I ask you to try what you could for me. I speak the Cree language well, and can trade with both the Chipe[w]yan and Salteaux in their own language…. I am sorry to have troubled you with so long a letter, but a drowning man will catch at a straw, and I am writing to you as a last chance.[2]

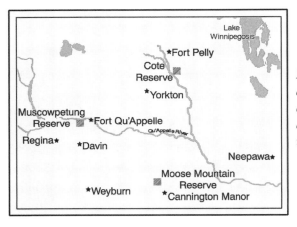

Native reserves associated with Halpin's career as an Indian agent. Weyburn is only a reference point.

When Halpin did not receive a reply, he wrote a second letter:

I am writing to you again to ask you is there any chance of my being employed by the HBC. The winter is close at hand and I would like to be sure of a berth of some sort. I have a chance of a position in the Indian Department, but I would like much better to be in the service of the Company in which I have spent so many years of my life. I know I have the good wishes of many of the Hudson's Bay officers. I would be glad if you would let me know soon what my chances are with the Company.[3]

Commissioner Wrigley advised him that he could not offer him anything at the time and that he had better take the position with Indian Affairs.[4] That being the case, Halpin did so. In November 1885, it was reported that he was appointed assistant Indian agent in Edmonton,[5] but it is not clear whether he took the position. He appears to have stayed in the Regina area.

In January 1886, at age 32, Henry Halpin married Annie Mariah Douglas Elliott, the daughter of Robert Wilson Elliott, the justice of the peace and political organizer for the Conservatives at nearby Balgonie.[6] Annie was a milliner, a women's hat maker, who had operated a shop in Brandon before she suffered a severe mental breakdown.[7] It is not known how Henry and Annie met, or how long they had known each other, but it is possible that they could have met in Brandon, or through his brother Charles who worked as a reporter for The Regina Leader, *whose editor Nicholas Flood Davin, was a close friend of Annie's father. Robert Elliott was also the postmaster for the village of Davin from 1890 to 1900. During the trial of Louis Riel, Charles Halpin, who was a member of the Manitoba Rifles, had guarded Riel. His editor, Davin, disguised as priest, had interviewed Riel the night before he was hanged.*

Within months of being hired by Indian Affairs, Henry Halpin was appointed clerk on the Muscowpetung Reserve near Fort Qu'Appelle, northeast of Regina. His salary was $720 per year.[8] When the Reverend George Bryce, historian and founder of Manitoba College, visited the Muscowpetung Reserve, he commented that Halpin was one of the best Cree interpreters he had encountered in his travels.[9]

The Muscowpetung Reserve had been created in July 1885 for the local Cree and Ojibwa who had remained loyal to the government during the Rebellion. One of the bands was led by Chief Piapot. The purpose of the reserve was to contain the Indians and provide them with a stable food supply by teaching them to farm. The depletion of bison herds that had been the staple food supply in the past, was one of the problems that had caused Poundmaker, an adopted Blackfoot but born Cree, and Big Bear's young men to join Riel's rebellion.

Occasionally The Regina Leader *commented on Halpin's work on the reserve: "Mr. H.R. Halpin of Muscowpetung's Reserve was in town last week. He says it would do you good to see the Indians working. They are fixing up their houses, hauling hay to the stables and generally preparing for winter. They of course know all about the 'Messiah Craze' which has got hold of their brethren across the border, but it does not affect them."[10]*

Chief Piapot, 1885.

Halpin made friends with a number of important people in the Regina area. One of them was a lawyer, Hugh A. Robson, who would later sit as a judge in Winnipeg. It was at Robson's home that Henry and Annie's second child, Eva, was born in 1888. Henry's friendship with Davin, who later became the local Member of Parliament, also increased. This may have had something to do with the fact that both of them had been born in County Limerick, Ireland. In 1890, Henry and Annie Halpin named the third of their eight children Nicholas Flood Davin Halpin.

Courtesy of the Glenbow Archives, NA–2883–23

Nicholas Flood Davin, MP.

Halpin's clerical work at Muscowpetung was recognized and in 1889 he was recommended by A.E. Forget, the assistant commissioner of Indian Affairs, for a promotion to a permanent position in the Department of Indian Affairs.[11] Halpin remained at the reserve until the summer of 1892 when he was transferred to the Pelly Agency, in eastern Saskatchewan, north of Yorkton, where there was a clerical vacancy.[12]

Soon after arriving at the new position Halpin realized that this move had been a mistake. The living conditions on the Cote Reserve near the Hudson's Bay Company Fort Pelly placed a great strain on Halpin, his pregnant wife, and family. A series of letters which Halpin wrote back to Regina to Hayter Reed, the commissioner of Indian Affairs, speak for themselves:

> During the cold weather of the last few days I find it quite impossible to live in my present quarters, at least [it is] for my wife and children. My wife has been, and is still in very poor health, and not able to stand the cold, and the many other drawbacks [?] with this place. Therefore I have decided to get them back to their friends at Balgonie until things are more comfortable here. I therefore beg to ask you for leave of absence from this place for three weeks. I would like to leave on the 8th February and could be back by the 28th or there about. I have never before during the seven years I have been with the Department asked for holidays. Therefore I hope you will grant my request as my family could not go the journey by themselves, there being four little children…. I will do my best to get on here and I think I will get on well with Mr. [William] Jones [the Indian agent].[13]

Halpin's leave of absence was granted[14] and he took his family to Balgonie, but Hayter Reed, an unsympathetic bureaucrat located in Regina and not necessarily familiar with the conditions, did not take Halpin's complaints seriously and made an assessment of him similar to what had been made by Halpin's HBC supervisors earlier. In a letter to Minister of the Interior J. Mayne Daly, Hayter Reed stated:

I am certainly unable to see Mr. Halpin has any just cause for complaint. There are plenty of men with families in the service who are stationed in places quite, if not more out of the way as Pelly, and are glad enough to hold their positions. The house is one that can be made sufficiently comfortable, and many good men in their country and in our service have had to content themselves with worse. Of course in the disposal of our men, we have to consider general before individual interests, and Mr. Halpin has not displayed any such merit as to entitle him to exceptional consideration. Mr. Lash under whom he served until removed from Muscowpetung felt that while Mr. Halpin to a certain point performed his service sufficiently satisfactorily, he could never relax his supervision of him, nor throw any responsibility on him. Mr. Jones, under whom he now serves, gives anything but favourable reports of him.[15]

In a more private letter written to the minister of the Interior that day, Hayter Reed said he felt that Halpin's:

complaints about Pelly are largely instigated by his wife, who is a generally dissatisfied, disconcerted soul. Jones [the Indian agent] gives a decidedly bad account of him, regards him as very useless outside of his ordinary routine clerical work, and does not consider him loyal to his superiors. He says he refers everything to Davin [the local MP] and I don't think that sort of thing on the part of men in our employ is conductive to discipline, being in contravention of the Department's express instructions against using political influence. This hardly seems to be the sort of men deserving of being allowed to pick and choose.[16]

When the department did nothing about the Halpin's living conditions the domestic strain increased. Anne Halpin refused to go back to the Cote

Reserve and took the children to Neepawa, Manitoba. She stayed there with relatives and awaited the birth of her fifth baby.
Again Henry Halpin wrote to Hayter Reed:

I beg to lay before you the following with regard to my position as clerk in Fort Pelly Agency with the hope that you will look favourably on my request. I find for the following reasons my position very hard. In the first place, my wife is in very poor health, and is often in need of medical aid, which is impossible to get here as the nearest doctor is at Yorkton 55 miles from here and, as you know, I was forced to take her away from this place last month.

We had a very hard time here this winter, our house being so very small and in such bad repair. It is a one-room concern 14 x 16 [ft.] inside and last fall after the snow came there were many times when my wife and little children could not stay in their beds [on account of] the snow and rain coming through the roof. My wife stood it as long as she possibly could, but her health suffered in the meantime. In second place, the nearest white women are ten miles away, which is also very hard on my wife and children. Again two of my children are of an age to attend school and there is no place where I can send them to, nearer than Yorkton. It is costing me nearly $10.00 per week to keep them there where they are now in Neepawa, and the expense is more than I can honestly stand.

I beg to refer you to Inspector Wadsworth as to the state of my quarters here. He saw them a few days ago. I therefore beg that you will transfer me to some other agency where I can have my family with me and where we will be in reach of a doctor if he is required. I have during my eight years service worked hard and loyally in the interests of the department. Trusting you will favour my request as soon as possible. I would be satisfied with any change from this Agency."[17]

Halpin's financial difficulties were serious. He was being paid $15.00 per week, and most of it was going for his family's room and board elsewhere. Even Annie Halpin wrote to Hayter Reed from Neepawa asking for a transfer for her husband:

> For the sake of the writer I hope you will take time to examine the contents of this letter. About two months ago we left Pelly Agency to visit my father at Davin, near Balgonie. The trip was an awful one from Pelly to Yorkton at that time of the year as we had to go by stage. My health was not good and it was impossible for us to remain any longer in the house we had to live in there. The rain or snow came down in many places in the sleeping room and the roof fell in, in the kitchen part. We certainly would have frozen had Mr. H. not kept on fires at night.
>
> The place might suit a bachelor but certainly is not a place for a family. Could you not change Mr. H. from there to Birtle where there would be a school for the children or he would be willing to go back to Muscowpetung? He has worked very hard up there where he is and deserves a change. We have many expenses we otherwise would not have. Could we have a house to go to? Do try Mr. Reed and change Mr. Halpin to Birtle or somewhere soon that he may have less expenses. The trial of so many little children is rather much for me, away from home and father. Our baby was very ill for a long time after the dreadful trip we had. For a time we thought he would not recover. Trusting to hear from you soon.[18]

The new baby, Charles Bernard Halpin, was born at Neepawa on April 22, 1893. Halpin was becoming desperate to be with his family. He had not seen his latest son and there was a great risk of his marriage breaking up. He wrote again to Hayter Reed:

Even at the risk of incurring your displeasure, I once more throw myself on your mercy, and ask you for a change from this Agency to another. I don't care where, if there would only be a house into which I can bring my family, even though I had to pay rent for it.

I am as you know an old timer in this country, and not the sort of man to kick about my habitation, but during the twenty-three years I have been in the Northwest, I never lived in a house anything like this. Logs rotten, all kinds of fungus growing on the inside walls, roof in the main part of the shanty leaking badly all over. Roof of lean-to falling in (and if not supported by props [would] have gave [way] long ago.) If I were alone I could pull through but with my wife and five children, it is simply impossible for me to live here. Our Indian servant girl left us last winter because she could not stand the cold in the house. What must it have been for my little children?

I would be quite willing, should you transfer me, to let part of my salary go monthly to pay the expenses of my transport.

My family [is] still at Neepawa and it costs me $10.00 every week to keep them boarding there and I am at the same [time] trying to pay Le Jeune what I owe him. If you cannot see your way to help me I will have to bring my family back here and risk it. Therefore if you could see your way towards a transfer from this [place] it would save me the expense of bringing them back here. I hope you will forgive me for again troubling you.[19]

In another letter the next day, Halpin added: "I am afraid I forgot to say in my last letter to you that I am quite willing to lose my rations etc. in the event of your transferring me to some other place. I would be willing to do or be anything elsewhere. There are very great reasons for my wishing to be moved from this place, which I don't care to write."[20]

Hayter Reed replied to Halpin's desperation:

I shall consider the matter thoroughly and possibly in the near future be able to act, but this cannot be done before a month, and consequently I would advise you not to take your family North until you again hear from me. I might state in this connection that I have authorized the agent to erect a nice little building for the Clerk.[21]

Halpin was thankful for Reed's reply, but was not happy in regards to his family:

I have received your kind letter and I am very grateful to you for the hope you give me of an exchange from this place, and should you see your way to transfer me, I will try and show you by renewed efforts to do well, and by working hard, how much I appreciate your kindness to me in this matter, which you, I am sure, is one of vital importance to me and my little children.

It is very hard on me just now having to pay so much to keep my family away from me. It costs me about $10.00 a week on the average, and has done so since March last, not counting doctor's bills. Therefore I ask you most respectfully to let me hear from you just as soon as possible, as to what I am to do with regard to my family.[22]

Sometime later Annie Halpin and the children joined Henry at the Cote Reserve even though there were no school facilities. Soon another family crisis arose when Hayter Reed temporarily sent him to the Shoal River Reserve near Pelican Rapids in western Manitoba. Annie apparently did not want him to go and he resigned rather than leave his family. A message was sent by Indian Agent Jones to Hayter Reed who telegraphed Jones to accept Halpin's resignation. After Halpin's sister, also named Annie and who was living in Neepawa at the time, promised to stay with his family, Henry rescinded his resignation and went to Shoal River with William Jones, the Indian agent.

In the meantime, Hayter Reed had accepted Halpin's resignation and transferred another clerk to the Pelly Agency. Halpin made plans to leave and wrote to Hayter Reed to explain his actions and to arrange an interview in Regina:

> I have the honour to acknowledge the receipt of your letter of the 13th instant No. 1760 and if possible will leave here en route from Regina on Wednesday the 27th instant, via Fort Qu'Appelle.
>
> I am quite sure that you did all in your power to help me in the matter of a transfer to some other point in the service of the Department, and had it been at all possible, I would have been quite willing to await your pleasure in the matter, but owing to the trouble I have with my family matters, I thought the only thing to do (and keep my reason) was to resign my position here, even at the risk of being thrown open the world with a large helpless family and no work.
>
> I told you last spring my reason for wishing a change. I have been too long knocking about the country to care anything for the pleasure or conveniences of a town, or even close to a settlement and were it not for my family, you could not send me too far from either.
>
> As to my refusing to go with the Indian agent to Shoal River, I was at my wits end about leaving my wife alone, while I was away, but on my sister promising to remain here till my return, I was quite willing to go and be of any service I could to Mr. Jones. This I think he will tell you yourself. Hoping you will give me one more chance in the service.[23]

William Jones, who had a certain amount of sympathy for Halpin's situation, also wrote to Hayter Reed:

I beg to state that Mr. Halpin rescinded his letter refusing to go to Shoal River and went with me there, doing his best to assist me.

A good deal of Mr. Halpin's action is caused I imagined by his wife who is not in the best of health. If he was situated differently and with [a] certain class of work he would do very well, but as I said before and as he acknowledges himself, he is not adapted for the class of work required of him at this Agency. He purposes seeing you. I hope that you will do what you can for him so as not to take the Bread and Butter from him.[24]

After taking his family to Regina, Halpin had difficulty finding work. In desperation he again appealed to Hayter Reed, who had been promoted to the position of deputy superintendent of Indian Affairs in Ottawa:

I ask you most respectfully that you will allow me to continue in the service of the Department for a short time as I am not in a position here in Regina and go to look for work. My wife has been very ill since we came to Regina and I could not well leave her here should I have to try and find work in any other part of the country.

I am very sorry now that I left Cote and had not Mr. Jones told me before I left that my resignation was not accepted, I don't think I would have come to Regina. I only ask that you give me employment for a time till I can find something else. You know how hard it is to find anything to do here in the winter. All my furniture, stoves, etc. is still at Pelly and I don't know when it will be here. I don't know anything else to say and throw myself on your mercy and ask for a few more months' employment till I can find something else. I have tried very hard to find employment here, but without anything turning up. I have been with the Dept. so long that I feel my position very much. I hope you will overlook for this time whatever I have had done to annoy you, for it was quite unintentional on my part. I would go most willingly to any place you might wish to send me and do my best to give satisfaction.[25]

It helped to have friends in high places. Davin may have had a hand in his re-appointment. Halpin was taken on by the Regina office by his former supervisor Amédée Emmanuel Forget, who had written good reports of him when he was at Muscowpetung. A.E. Forget was now the commissioner of Indian Affairs.[26] It was while living in Regina that Halpin wrote the sixteen-page memoir of his captivity in 1885 and gave it to fellow clerk, J.R.C. Honeyman for editing, with the idea that it would be published.[27]

Things worked out well for Halpin in the Regina office. Forget, who would later become the lieutenant-governor of the North-West Territories (and later Saskatchewan) and a senator, was happy with Halpin. He wrote to Hayter Reed: "He [Halpin] appears to be doing his best and I am quite satisfied with his work."[28]

When a clerical position came open at the Moose Mountain Agency in March 1894, Forget was only too happy to recommend Halpin for that position. "This is very fortunate for him and his family as he had not been able to secure another position."[29] Hayter Reed concurred and approved Halpin's transfer.[30]

14 Moose Mountain Agency

*T*he Moose Mountain Agency, to which Henry Halpin was appointed clerk, was located in southeastern Saskatchewan. The Halpins lived at nearby Cannington Manor, the famous colony of transplanted middle-class Brits who sought to be gentlemen farmers and who entertained themselves with their cricket matches, rugby games, horse racing, and fox hunts. The Cannington community had been started by the Moose Mountain Trading Company in 1882. Besides the houses, the village had a variety of shops, several mills, a town hall/school, and an Anglican church. A twenty-room mansion, after which the community was named, was several miles to the southwest. The community did not thrive after the proposed railway route was changed to the south.[1] The Halpin family's sojourn at Cannington Manor was during the village's declining years. It is not clear how Annie Halpin liked her new surroundings, but she appears to have spent considerable time away from the area. She was back in Neepawa, Manitoba, where Henry's sister lived, on April 3, 1897, when their son Robert was born there.

The Moose Mountain Agency consisted of three separate reserves of about the same size: Pheasant Rump's Band was Assiniboine, Striped Blanket's Band was mostly Assiniboine with some Cree, while White Bear's Band was Cree and Salteaux.

Henry Halpin apparently thrived at the Moose Mountain Agency. In his 1896 annual report, Indian Agent J.J. Campbell noted: "Mr. Halpin

Remains of Cannington Manor. Photo by the author, 2004.

still fills the position of agency clerk satisfactorily, and has his time fully occupied by the duties of his position."[2]

After Campbell resigned in 1897, Henry Halpin was placed in charge of the Moose Mountain Agency. His official title was "Farmer in Charge."[3] *One of his main duties was to facilitate the enforced transition of the Natives from a migratory hunting, trapping, and gathering economy to that of a more sedentary existence as ranchers and farmers. The skills in gardening, farming, and fishing that he had learned during his Hudson's Bay Company years at Norway House and Oxford House began to pay off. By July 1900, his yearly salary was had grown to $900.*[4]

Henry Halpin's annual reports to the Department of Indian Affairs give a glimpse into his work and his own attitudes. Even under Halpin's benign administration the Natives lived under a state of paternalism; those who were formerly lords of the plains, were now treated as children, wards of the state. His reports were very detailed, providing information on Native culture, the problems of dry-land farming, the role of Christian missionaries on the reserves, as well as reflecting his understanding of Native feelings about the hated residential schools. The statistical information that he supplied, indicates that the death rate among those under his care generally exceeded the birth rate.

To demonstrate his position, information is taken from his comments about White Bear's Band, No. 70, the reserve that he directly supervised. His report for 1897 reads:

This reserve is situated in the south-east part of the Moose Mountain, with an area of thirty-thousand seven hundred and twenty acres. A large portion of the reserve is covered with poplar wood and lakes, in some of which pike, pickerel and suckers are caught. Most of the Indian houses and fields are situated on the south-eastern part of the reserve, the land being more level and better adapted for farming and stock raising, there being good shelter in the small bluffs for the stables, and numerous small lakes where the cattle can be watered without having far to drive them, which is of great importance during our long cold winters.

The Indians depend in a great measure upon the sale of dry fire wood and logs (fire killed), which they cut and sell to the white settlers. They are also beginning to reap some benefit from their cattle, and from the produce of their farms and gardens.

The band at present numbers one hundred and twenty-six souls, made up of thirty men, thirty-nine women and fifty-six children. During the year there were six births and thirteen deaths. Most of the deaths were of children under five years of age and the principal causes were la grippe [influenza] and consumption.

There was an epidemic of la grippe among the Indians last spring, which caused many deaths among the children before it was stamped out. The vaccination of the Indians was as usual attended to last fall, at the annuity payments, and every other sanitary precaution possible is given due attention.

Besides farming and cattle-raising and the sale of wood and logs already referred to, these Indians gain much of their support from the tanning of cow-hides, horse-hides, and dog and sheep skins for the settlers in the district round about their reserve. The Indians dress these skins in the same way they used to do the buffalo robes in the old days, and some of the women do beautiful work and make the cow-robes as white and soft as a blanket. They are well paid for their work by the white people, who do not appear to be able to do this kind of work.

During the fall the women gather and sell large quantities of wild fruit. The digging and sale of senega-root is also a source of income to them.

Very little fur is caught now in this district, and the Indians do not count much on it. The white settlers in the neighbourhood give some of the working men and women good wages and employ them often in their houses and also at harvest. The earnings of the band during the year amounted to more than $2,000.

The Indians worked very well at haying last year and put up nearly five hundred tons of hay, and after feeding their cattle well all winter, had a good quantity of hay left over in the spring, and there are still at this date some Indians with hay for sale. They had a very fair crop of wheat last fall, which provided them with a good deal of flour, and also seed for their land this spring. Their gardens yielded well, as did also their potatoes and turnips. Indians do not care to eat potatoes, and it is difficult to get them to plant any quantity of that vegetable, there being very little sale for them to the settlers. They are beginning to take more interest in their gardens and attend to the weeding of them better than formerly, but there is still great room for improvement in this respect. A few Indians hauled some manure on to their fields this spring, and I hope to get others to do the same this fall after harvest.

The herd now numbers one hundred and nineteen head. There were twelve head sold and consumed by the Indians during the year, and the casualties were only four. None of the Indians have been milking their cows regularly and I do not think they ever will until they give up their summer tent life, and stay in their houses the year around. All the cattle wintered well and are now in fine condition, and I have arranged for the sale of some of them to a cattle-buyer and obtained the best price that is being paid in this district. I am sorry to say that the Indians as well as the white settlers in this district have had a poor return for their herd in the way of calves this spring, there being only an increase of three calves from thirty cows. This complaint is general in the district and the farmers can give me no satisfactory explanation as to the cause; I am glad to say, however, that when making my visits to the Indian herd, I noticed that a large proportion of the cows and heifers are in calf and I hope in the fall to be able to report a good increase in the number of calves.

Some of the Indians in this band have much better houses than they are living in at present. New buildings are in the course of erection, which when finished, will add much to the comfort of the Indians, being much larger, and with an upper storey in some of them. They will be shingled and plastered with lime and sand and have good windows and doors.

There are twenty-five children of school age in the band, and seven of them are attending the industrial schools at Regina, Qu'Appelle and Elkhorn. It is very difficult to get the parents to allow the children to be sent away to school, more especially those Indians who are in any [way] connected with the deposed chief White Bear[5] and his sons, who will have nothing to do with anything in the shape of education, and who try to live as they did before treaty was made with the North-West Indians, and they will hardly allow any one to talk on the subject of education to them, and simply say that their "God" did not intend them to be educated like white people; they will not allow that there would be any benefit to be derived from having their children taught, and say they would much prefer to see their little ones dead than at school.

There are one hundred and sixteen pagans in this band, and ten who profess to belong to one or other of Christian denominations. The Presbyterian Church has started a mission on this reserve, which is now in [the] charge of Mr. F.T. Dodds, who came here last spring most highly recommended by the Reverend Dr. Baird, and I feel confident that he will do good work among these people, in which he will be ably assisted by his wife. Mr. Dodds also visits Pheasant Rump's and Striped Blanket's Bands as often as possible. He has as interpreter one of the boys who were educated at the Regina industrial school.

These Indians are beginning to show a little more interest in their work, but they still require constant supervision; they seem to forget what is said to them so easily, and have not yet acquired the habit of looking ahead, and are at ease so long as they have a dollar in their possession. They are law abiding, and there has been no charge brought against any of them during the past year.

I regret to say that there was one case of drunkenness on the reserve during the past year. The Indian was punished by the late agent for the offense, and I trust that no more cases will occur, though I fear some few people in the settlement are not quite careful enough in respect to giving liquor to Indians. No immoral intercourse with white men has come under my notice.

The staff in this agency has been reduced by half, Mr. W. [William] Murison, who acted as interpreter and managed the Indians at their work under the late agent, is now living on the western reserves and has Pheasant Rump's and Striped Blanket's Bands under his care. These bands were until lately looked after by Mr. Lawford, whose services were dispensed with. I feel confident that Mr. Murison will bring these Indians on well; he is young and enthusiastic and takes a great interest in anything he undertakes. He got the Indians together last year and started a football team, which has done very well under his guidance, and in one or two matches which they played with local white teams they came out pretty well. The Indians themselves take a great interest in their games, and the ball is seldom at rest during their spare time, and on one occasion last fall they got up a match among themselves and were so taken up with the game that they played all night before either side would allow itself beaten and give up.

The whole of the work on White Bear's reserve, both office and in connection with the farming, is done by myself. I also oversee the work on the western reserves.[6]

Halpin's report for 1898 contained additional reflections on improvements in the Natives' economy and the progress in education and Christianization.

The men attend to the usual farm work during the summer, and in the winter they find their time fully occupied hauling hay and attending to their cattle, cutting and hauling dry logs and firewood for sale, making hayracks, bob-sleighs and jumpers. A few of them do a little trapping and hunting; but as very little fur is caught now in this district, they do not stick to it for any length of time, and prefer some other work at which they are sure of making something. They put up last summer the largest quantity of hay ever put up on the reserve, and after feeding their stock well during the winter, had a great deal to sell this spring.

Fifty-eight acres of new land have been broken since the snow went away, and I hope to have at least one hundred acres of new land ready for crop next spring; about four miles of new fence has been built, and about one hundred loads of manure put on the fields.

The grain crop last fall was a failure and the Indians got very little benefit from it; the yield of root crops was also very much below average. The poor yield was in a great measure owing to the poor state of the land, which had been used for years without rest, and no attempt made to better it, by manuring, or summer-fallowing. This season they have in the largest crop ever put in on the reserve, some of it on new breaking, and the prospects of a good yield are encouraging.

The department kindly gave me authority to purchase some seed potatoes from the Experimental farm at Indian Head, Saskatchewan, and I am in hopes of being able next spring to make a change of seed potatoes all round. The varieties sown are the "Polaris," "Everett," and "Empire State," which were recommended by Mr. McKay of the Experimental farm. The Indian gardens are looking well.

The herd now numbers one hundred and fifty-five head, an increase of thirty-six since this time last year; and during the year the Indians killed for beef, and sold, seventeen head. The cattle were never better attended to than they were last winter, and the increase in young stock this spring is very satisfactory. The cattle belonging to this band are extra good; all the bulls used here have been thoroughbred [purebred] pedigreed animals, and we always get the highest price from cattlemen for any we may have for sale.

The Indians are showing much more interest in their cattle than they did, and there are a few Indians on the reserve now, anxious to own cattle, who previously have refused them.

The buildings are about the same as last year. Three new houses and two stables have been built during the year; the stables are an improvement on the old ones, being higher.

There are twenty-five children of school age in the band, and seven of them are attending the industrial schools at Qu'Appelle and Elkhorn.

Out of the number still on the reserve and not going to school, I think there are three who would pass the doctor's examination as being fit to be placed in an industrial school; the remainder are more or less the victims of scrofula [a condition which produces tumours] and other kindred diseases, and would not, under the present regulations, be received in any boarding or industrial institution.

I am pleased to say that Old White Bear, since his reinstatement by the Department as chief, has not been so much against having the children educated, but he still holds back with regard to allowing them to be sent far from home to school.

The Indians of this band are for the most part pagans. The Presbyterian Church has a mission on this reserve in charge of Mr. T.F. Dodds who has been here for over a year, and he is well thought of by the Indians, who always receive him pleasantly in their houses, and listen with patience to what he says to them. There is no church on the reserve, and no regular services are held, but Mr. Dodds makes house-to-house visits, and reads to them from the Bible in their own language; Mr. Dodds is making good progress in the Indian language, and now after only one year can make himself well understood by the Indians. Both he and his wife are kind and patient with the Indians under all circumstances, and never tire in helping them in any way possible. They have visited the sick from day to day, Mrs. Dodds taking with her on her visits any little luxury in the way of food that she thought would help the sick. The work and life of such people as Mr. and Mrs. Dodds must, and I doubt not, will, have a good effect upon the Indians, though it may be a long time before there are any signs of the good work going on. Mr. Dodds has given many of the Indians Bibles printed in their own language, and there are many of them that can read very well.

I am glad to be able to say that the progress of these Indians during the year has been marked. In their houses one can see the progress made, nearly every house has ordinary beds, and every house but one has a good lumber floor. They are as a rule kept clean and neat. The doors are properly hung on iron hinges, and windows, in most cases, have been well put in.

Red Star and Shewack both bought new lumber wagons last fall, from the proceeds of cattle sold by them; Notchokao and Mus-quah-kah-ween-apit bought a mower in partnership. Lone Child bought a fine set of double harness to enable him to use his ponies while hay-making. He also bought a second-hand wagon from a settler in the neighbourhood. He now owns a mower, horse-rake, wagon and sleighs, and has twenty-three head of private cattle.

Shewack has twenty-five head of cattle, and Red Star seventeen head. The following Indians have broken over ten acres of new land this season: Lone Child, Red Star, John and Fred Waywinche. Kappo, Shewack and Ka-ka-ke-way have broken between them about nine acres; some others have done a little breaking, and all are looking forward to a large acreage for next year. There has been no charge brought against any of these Indians during the year.

Taken altogether the Indians of this band are quiet and orderly; there are, however, a few exceptions, but I hope by firmness and kind treatment, they will come round with the more respectable members of the band. I do not know of any immoral intercourse with white men, but I fear they are not so strict among themselves.

All the Indians under my charge are contented and are advancing towards civilization and self-support, and visitors to the reserve wonder at the upward step they have made during the past year, especially on White Bear's reserve. Old White Bear since his reinstatement as chief has done all in his power to get his sons to work on the reserve, with the result that two of them are amongst my best workers.

Inspector McGibbon visited the agency in January last, and I think was pleased with what he saw, and his kind and encouraging words to the Indians have had the effect of making many of them work better than they might otherwise have done....

In conclusion, I beg to thank the department for the assistance in the way of new implements and seed grain given these Indians this spring, and without which they could not have put in a crop of any kind. The Indians appreciate what the department has done, and it has had a good effect upon them. I would say that no effort has been spared on my part to carry out the instructions of the department, at the same time the interests of the Indians have been attended to."[7]

The inspector of Indian reserves was favourably impressed with Halpin's work and wrote: "The office work was correctly done and the inventory showed careful management, Mr. Halpin was proving himself to be a successful agent, and he was ably assisted by Mr. Murison."[8] Halpin's report for 1899 mentioned the agricultural and social progress made by the Natives under his care.

The band at present numbers one hundred and twenty-three, a decrease of three since this time last year; there are twenty-nine men, thirty-seven women, and fifty-seven children. There were seven births and ten deaths during the year. Grippe was the cause of most of the deaths.

The general health of the band for the most of the year was good, but an epidemic of grippe gave a lot of trouble this spring, and at one time there were over seventy cases, more or less severe, on the reserve. All the usual sanitary measures, such as cleaning up all filth and rubbish in and around the Indian houses, were well looked after, and everything that would burn was burned. The majority of houses were whitewashed, both inside and out.

There is an abundance of hay, and a large area of timberland on the reserve. There is also a large lake, White Bear's, where the Indians catch a good quantity of fish in season. In favourable seasons wild fruit of all kinds is to be had in large quantities, for which the Indians receive good payment in the village of Cannington and from the white people in the neighbourhood. In the winter a large quantity of dry fire-wood and building logs is cut for sale. The women tan hides and other skins for settlers and get well paid for their work.

Mixed farming and the raising of cattle are the principal occupations of this band, and I am glad to say that the Indians have begun to show a great interest in their work.

The men have their time fully taken up during the spring and summer with the usual farm work at that time of the year, and in the winter they have their cattle to look after; they have most of them to haul their hay a long way to their stables, and it takes the best part of a day in winter to get home a load of hay from the hay lands seven miles away from their stables. They also cut a lot of fire-wood and building logs, which they sell to the settlers in the district. This spring they have a good acreage in wheat and other grain, about one hundred and forty-acres altogether, and they also built about eight miles of new fence around the cultivated lands. They have broken eighty-four acres of new land since this time last year, and I expect to have a good deal more land broken up before fall. The acreage under crop this year is over eighty acres more than last year, and an increase of over one hundred acres since the year before. The women of the band attend to the usual housework, tan hides, pick berries, and dig senega-root for sale; they also do a good deal of fishing, weed gardens and do other such work.

The grain crop last fall was the best they ever had, over seventeen hundred bushels of grain was threshed, and though the crop of roots was small, all was of good quality. The crop at present looks first-rate and there is every prospect of a bountiful harvest. The gardens and root crops are a little backward, but with a few warm dry days I think they will be all right. It is going to be harder work this year than formerly to get our hay, owing to the high water in all the hay sloughs. I have never seen such a quantity of water in the sloughs on the prairies as there is this year since away back in the early seventies when I first came to the Northwest, but the upland hay will be a good crop this year, and as we shall have a large quantity of straw, our stock will not suffer.

The herd now numbers one hundred and fifty-eight head, and all are in good condition. The increase in calves this year is satisfactory. All the Indians looked after their stock very well during the winter. Eight young heifers were purchased by the Indians to replace some of those killed or sold last fall.

The buildings on the reserve are much the same as last year. A few new houses and stables have been built.

There are twenty-four children of school age on the reserve, and of this number eight are attending the industrial schools at Qu'Appelle and Elkhorn. Since White Bear was reinstated as chief, the Indians of this band have been asking for a school on the reserve, and when the Deputy Superintendent General visited the reserve last fall the Indians asked him for a school, and he promised to do what he could for them. I am sure that were a school opened, there would be no trouble in getting children to attend. There are a number of children on the reserve who would not be received at an industrial school, owing to their suffering from scrofula, and other diseases of a like nature, but were a day school started on the reserve, I think it would help the industrial schools in the future, for the teacher in the day school could see that the children in attendance were washed every day and kept clean, which is more than half the battle where scrofula is the trouble. In this way, after a year or so, there would, I think be some children fit to be sent off the reserve to school.

The Indians of this band are for the most part pagans. During the past year, however, some few have shown some interest in the teachings of the Reverend Mr. Dodds, our missionary. Both Mr. and Mrs. Dodds have been indefatigable in their work on the reserve, and I can see that the Indians have respect for them, and look upon them as friends. On two or three occasions when there were deaths on the reserve the Indians sent for Mr. Dodds and asked him to perform a Christian burial service at the grave; this, I think shows that there is a better feeling working in some of them in the matter of religion, for I know it is only a very short time ago when such a thing would have been impossible even were the Indians paid for it.

This band has made good progress during the years. I mention the following names of what is being done:

Red Star last year had three acres in wheat; this season, thirty-three acres. John [?], last year, wheat, five acres; this year sixteen. Lone Child, last year, wheat, four acres; this year sixteen. F. Waywinche Kappo, last year, no crop; this year sixteen acres of wheat alone. I could mention many others who have done well, and all show more taste for work than formerly, and I think they are beginning to see and feel that it is the man who works that is best off. Several new wagons were purchased during the year, as was also horse harness of good quality.

There has been a good deal of help in the way of food given this band during the year, but if our harvest this fall comes anywhere near what it should be, the issue of food for the coming year will be small.

It is now only on very rare occasions I see an Indian with a painted face, and most of the people dress in white people's clothes, and have put aside the blanket.

The earnings of the band during the year were in the neighbourhood of $3,000, which was properly spent.

The general behaviour of the band has been good. Only one attempt was made to hold a "sun dance" during the year, and I am glad to say I had very little trouble in putting a stop to it.[9] I do not think the Indians will ever try to hold one here again. Mr. Murison continues in charge of Pheasant Rump and Striped Blanket Bands, and works hard to bring them on.

Being quite alone here, I find my time fully occupied from day to day, and have no spare moments; but the great advance towards civilization and self-support made by these Indians during the past two years encourages me to still further exertions to bring them on.

I thank the department very much, on behalf of the Indians under my care, for the great help given them in the way of farming implements.[10]

The agricultural progress of the White Bear Reserve was again noted in Halpin's report for 1900, but the size of the band continued dropping through disease and a low birth rate. Little had been done by the Department of Indian Affairs in regard to Halpin's suggestion that a school be established on the reserve. Again he was asking for more help in managing the agency.

This reserve is situated in the southeast part of Moose Mountain eight miles from Cannington Manor ... and is well suited for mixed farming.

The band at present numbers one hundred and eighteen souls, a decrease of five since this time last year. There are twenty-eight men, thirty-seven women, twenty-nine boys, and twenty-four girls belonging to the band. There were seven deaths and two births during the year. Measles was the cause of most of the deaths. White Bear, the chief, died at the ripe age of ninety-seven.

The health of the band, apart from the epidemic of measles, was fairly good. All sanitary measures were attended to as far as possible, and when the Indians moved into their tents in the spring they left their houses in a clean and tidy condition, having burned all rubbish that collected on the premises during the winter.

The Indians of this reserve have the best hay lands in the district, and it will be a great source of profit to them this year, as the hay crop in the adjoining settlements will be a comparative failure....

The acreage under crop this year is about two hundred and fourteen, an increase of sixty-six acres over last year. We had a good return from our grain fields last fall, having threshed nearly three thousand bushels of grain on this reserve. At the present the prospects for a good crop this year are very slight, owing to the long-continued drought, but should we get rain within the next few days we may possibly get back enough for seed next spring, which is more than the majority of the white settlers in this district are going to do. Our hay lands are in fine condition, and what we lose in grain we shall more than make up in hay.

The cattle and horses on the reserve at present number one hundred and fifty-three head; this does not include the ponies, which are the private property of the Indians. Some oxen were exchanged for horses during the year, and these are now classed as "stock under government control," in the same way as the cattle for which they were exchanged. The Indians killed for their own consumption and sold during the year thirty-four head of cattle. The casualties were few. These Indians, with few exceptions, take good care of their cattle, and keep the stables comfortable, and well supplied with hay.

The buildings are much the same as last year.

There are twenty-four children of school age on the reserve, seven of whom are attending the industrial schools at Qu'Appelle or Elkhorn.

The Indians of the band are for the most part pagans, but the Reverend F.T. Dodds, who labours with them in the interests of the Presbyterian Church, informs me that he can notice a change for the better going on with some of them, and if kindness and patience can work a change in an Indian, both Mr. Dodds and his good wife should be rewarded with the conversion of the whole band.

This band has made good progress during the year towards self-support. The Indians received only one hundred pounds of flour from the department since last September.

One of the band, Red Star, threshed seven hundred and ninety bushels of No. 1 hard wheat last fall, and many others between two and three hundred bushels. Twelve good work horses were purchased during the year, and they are being made good use of.

A painted Indian is very seldom seen, and the sun dance is a thing of the past, so far as my Indians are concerned, and I have not heard it mentioned even this year. This is a step in the right way, for if there was one thing that tended more than another to keep the Indians back, it was and is the sun dance.

Several new sets of team harness have been purchased during the year and they are well taken care of. The band earned during the year over $5,000. The general behaviour of the band has been good.

I feel encouraged at the progress made in the agency during the past year, and it has been only by constant and hard work that this progress has been made. The change for the better is most noticeable on White Bear's reserve. Three years ago these Indians had about fifteen acres under crop; they have over two hundred acres this year, and are still breaking up new land. As I am quite alone here, my time is fully taken up with my work, both in the office and on the farm.

Last year was the first in the history of the agency that a supplementary estimate for flour did not have to be sent to the department.[11]

Halpin's plea for additional help became more urgent when on December 9, 1900, his wife Annie died of meningitis at Cannington Manor and was buried in the Church of England cemetery there.[12] She was 41 years of age. Because their youngest child Annie Rossine (Rosie) was less than a year old, Henry found it difficult to do his work and raise their eight children, only two of whom were teenagers. Little Rosie went to live with Henry's brother Nicholas and his wife Louisa in Brandon for several years.[13]

In March 1901, the Moose Mountain Agency underwent a radical reorganization due to government duplicity. As the surrounding white neighbours saw the progress of the Natives they became envious of their herds and land, and repeatedly petitioned the Minister of the Interior to sell them the reserve land. In violation of the terms and spirit of Treaty No. 4[14] the government rationalized the smaller reserves of the Moose Mountain Agency, amalgamating the two smaller bands, and transferring them to White Bear's reserve. The former smaller reserves were then sold, the government promising to protect the Native burials on the former reserves by placing iron fences around their cemeteries. Some of the proceeds of the

Cannington Manor Anglican Church and cemetery. Photo by the author, 2004.

land sales would be credited to the Natives' account. In effect, the original agency was reduced to about a third of its size and the population density of White Bear's reserve was almost doubled. This was the first of many reserve rationalizations that took place across the plains.[15]

Indian Commissioner David Laird came to Cannington Manor to close the deal. Henry Halpin was a party to this action, serving as an interpreter for the Cree and Saulteaux speakers during the surrender of their reserves. His assistant Murison was the interpreter for the Assiniboine. The Natives, themselves, had no independent counsel looking after their interests! Halpin's annual report for 1901 reflected upon the changes that had taken place:

Since my last report, the three bands in this agency, namely, Pheasant Rump, No. 68, Striped Blanket, No. 69, and White Bear's, No. 70, have been amalgamated, and all are now living on the reserve of the last-named band, the reserves that were formerly occupied by Pheasant Rump and Striped Blanket's bands having been surrendered to the department in March last, when the Indian Commissioner visited this agency. I will therefore include all three bands in my report on White Bear's reserve....

The population of this agency is at present one hundred and ninety-four, being an increase of one since my last annual report. The tribes are represented in the agency, namely, Cree, Saulteaux, and Assiniboine.

The health of these Indians on the whole has been fairly good. The sanitary regulations laid down by the department are attended to, and the homes of the Indians are in most cases kept clean and tidy. They give more attention to cleanliness, both of their persons and premises, than formerly, and appear to realize the necessity of cleanliness in their homes, which no doubt assists to ward off disease of a contagious nature. At the same time there is much room for improvement. I am glad to state that no epidemic visited these Indians during the year. Dr. J.G. Hardy, of Cannington Manor, is the medical officer for the agency, and he spares no pains and trouble to relieve those who are suffering. All who required vaccination were operated upon by him during the past year, and though smallpox has been in the vicinity of the reserve for some time, there have so far been no cases among the Indians, and the doctor informs me that the Indians are in a much better position with regard to smallpox than the majority of the white settlers, most of whom are not, or were not, until lately, vaccinated. I do not think two per cent of the Indians in this agency remain unvaccinated at the present time....

The crop of grain last year was a failure on the reserve, as well as with the majority of the white settlers in the vicinity of the reserve....

When here last March the Indian Commissioner promised these Indians a day school on the reserve, and all the Indians are looking forward to being able to get their children educated without sending them away from home.

These Indians are well supplied with the necessary farming implements. Mr. Murision, who is getting to be a capable blacksmith, keeps the tools in good repair. Binders were stored in the implement-shed during the winter.

The Presbyterian Church has a mission on the reserve conducted by Mr. F.T. Dodds. The Indians are always respectful to the missionary, and appear glad to have him visit them in their homes, where he reads to them out of the Bible in their own language; but most of the Indians are pagans, and do not even pretend otherwise, and attend all the different Indian dances that take place on the reserve.

Every year there are old houses pulled down and new ones of a better quality built in their places. After the death of the old chief, White Bear, last year, all the Indians moved to another part of the reserve, away from the place where the chief died, and put up sixteen new dwelling-houses, and as many stables. Most of the houses are of a better class than the ones they formerly occupied, though there is still much room for improvement. The crop being so poor last fall, the Indians were unable to purchase lumber for floors of their houses, and many of them had to go without in consequence. Should our crop be good this fall, there will not be many of the houses on the reserve without a lumber floor.

The Indians in this agency are improving in many ways, as, for instance, much of the money they earn, and derive from the sale of cattle, is spent in the purchase of wagons, mowers, rakes, and other articles of use; clothing, lumber, and shingles are also purchased and many articles which increase their household comfort. As a rule these Indians are a very law-abiding class of people. There was only one case during the year where the law had to step in and take away one of our young men for a term in jail at Regina, and I regret to say that this man was our only graduate from the Regina industrial school.

Some of these Indians who had nothing a few years ago have now a considerable number of cattle and horses and other personal property in the shape of wagons, sleighs, mowers, and such like. The majority of these Indians are less indolent than they were, and they find that they must work on their reserve if they want to get along, for the hunting of fur-bearing animals is a thing of the past in this agency.

The Indians are becoming better off each year, and are making steady progress in farming by increasing their fields and herds of cattle.

I can say that the Indians of this agency, as a whole, are industrious and law-abiding, and many are becoming better off each year, and had last season's crop not been a failure, we should not have required much assistance from the department this spring.

I have no trouble in preventing the introduction of intoxicants among these Indians, and have had to deal with only one case of drunkenness in four years. The Indians in the agency are moral, so far as white men are concerned, but I am afraid among themselves they are not so strictly virtuous as the department would like.

The crops were all well put in this spring, and the weather has been most favourable, so that the prospects are bright for a bountiful harvest. The agency was visited in March last by the Indian Commissioner, and during this visit the Indians in the western reserves surrendered their lands to the government and all are now living on the eastern or White Bear's reserve. All the Indians seem to get along without any friction, and all have worked well, and every bit of land has been put under crop.

No attempt was made to hold a sun dance last year, nor has such a thing been ever mentioned this season. This I consider a great stride towards civilization.

The earnings this year, apart from the sale of cattle, were much above the average, and though, as I said before, our crops were a failure, the Indians did not suffer from want of either food or clothing. I trust that each year will show greater advancement towards self-support on the part of these Indians and now that they are all together on one reserve, the progress should be marked.[16]

That was the last annual report that Henry Halpin submitted to the Department of Indian Affairs. The report of the inspector of reserves noted that Halpin had retired from the service of Indian Affairs during July 1901 (he was forty-seven years of age), and that he was temporarily replaced by his assistant Murison.[17] Halpin's retirement may have had a lot to do with the fact that he needed more time to spend with his young family, now that he was a widower.

Within the Indian Agency inspector's report is an undercurrent that suggests that Halpin's retirement may have been forced. He reported that Halpin's accounting of the cattle on the reserve was higher than an actual headcount showed. He noted that no new ground had been broken nor had summer-fallowing had been done. He also commented that the new homes and stables were not up to snuff.[18] When one considers that amount of work that Halpin had to do with the amalgamation of the three reserves into one, those comments may have been unjust.

193

In spite of his sanguine hopes for the future of the Moose Mountain Agency, Henry Halpin may not have been happy with what had occurred with the agency rationalization. He had made great progress towards developing Native economic self-sufficiency. The amalgamation of the reserves made for nothing all of the work the western bands had done in breaking their land and developing their crops. Now they had to start all over again, breaking more ground and building new houses. The increased population density of White Bear's reserve would put increased economic pressures on the band, preventing them from developing economic self-sufficiency and freedom from the Indian Act.[19] *The amalgamation of three different linguistic and cultural groups of Natives would have also created social tensions.*

Subsequent annual reports from the Moose Mountain Agency show that the promised day school was created on the reserve and the Presbyterian missionary was holding weekly services that the Natives attended.[20] However, all was not well and the transplanted chiefs became vocal, protesting further government reductions on the size of the reserve. Later, the residents of the reserve were able to acquire additional land, but they had to buy it from the government.

15 Fort Alexander and Epilogue

*A*fter he left the Department of Indian Affairs in 1901, Henry Halpin's movements are obscure during the next two years. In June 1903, he re-entered the service of the Hudson's Bay Company and was posted as a clerk to Fort Alexander, about eighty miles northeast of Winnipeg. He started with a month-to-month contract; his salary was $360 per year with board. By July 1903, his salary had been raised to $480 per year, but still considerably less than the $900 per year he had earned with Indian Affairs.[1]

At Fort Alexander, Halpin purchased fur, wood, and fish from the Natives. He shipped these products by barge to Winnipeg and other Hudson's Bay Company posts.[2] His employment evaluation later that year said that he is "very conscious to please."[3]

However, HBC correspondence shows that Henry Halpin was not well and had to take time off.[4] Late in November 1903 he had to take another leave of absence to go to Brandon. His brother Nicholas had died and it was necessary for him to go to make arrangements for the care of his own four-year-old daughter Annie Rossine who had been living with Nicholas and his wife.[5]

On February 1, 1904, Henry Halpin married his housekeeper, Flora Isabella Leask (1875–1972), a beautiful Métis woman who was twenty-one years his junior. They appear to have had a happy marriage and had four children, adding to Henry's eight from his earlier marriage to Annie.[6]

Another of Halpin's duties at Fort Alexander was service as a postal contractor for the Canadian Postal Service. When the man who was delivering the mail was ill, Halpin could not find a replacement. He could not do it himself because he too was ill; therefore he resigned from the postal position in July 1904.[7] His 1904 Hudson's Bay Company employment evaluation mirrored what his previous employers had said about him: "requires supervision."[8] In 1905, his eldest daughter Eva joined the Company in Winnipeg.[9]

Courtesy of Flora (Halpin) Ross

Flora (Leask) Halpin.

In 1907, Halpin's salary was raised to $600.00 per year with board. He remained with the Hudson's Bay Company at Fort Alexander until August 18, 1909, when he was terminated for "unsatisfactory service."[10] He was now at the age of fifty-five.

As a result of his termination the Halpins moved to nearby Poplar Park where Henry began farming.[11] Only one of his sons, Charles, took up farming as a career until 1916. Four of the other sons from the first marriage worked for the railway.[12]

In the First World War four of Henry's sons from his first marriage enlisted. Arthur was declared medically unfit. Jack deserted from Camp Hughes, southwest of Winnipeg, after two weeks of training.[13] Robert and Charles went overseas. Robert was discharged as medically unfit after having a kidney removed in England. Charles saw action on the continent, but died in Belgium from pneumonia following a bout of influenza on January 30, 1919.[14] Two of Henry and Flora's sons served their country during the Second World War.

Through his connections Henry Ross Halpin was appointed as a justice of the peace, a position he held until 1926.[15] He was also employed as a school inspector, possibly a patronage appointment. Later the Halpins moved into Winnipeg. Occasionally he visited his former Hudson's Bay Company boss from Fort Pitt and fellow prisoner

Courtesy of Flora (Halpin) Ross

Flora and Henry Halpin with their baby.

in 1885, W.J. McLean, who he said was the bravest man he knew. "He didn't know the meaning of fear."[16]

197

During his final years Henry gave a number of interviews to the press concerning his career. In an interview, in 1900, he predicted that the Moose Mountain Indians would be soon self-sufficient and he was proud of their success.[17] Interestingly, in all the published interviews that he did between 1905 and 1930, he never once mentioned his employment as an Indian agent, which suggests that that period in his life had been very painful and disappointing, as much of his positive work for the Natives had been undone by politicians and bureaucrats. The interviews suggested that he had been employed continuously by the Hudson's Bay Company.

This was the time that Henry Halpin wrote his longer memoir and sent it to his friend Judge H.A. Robson for examination.[18] In 1930, the *Manitoba Free Press* published a chapter of his memoir about his captivity, where he again exonerated Big Bear.[19]

When Henry Halpin died on Winnipeg on May 5, 1930, the front page of the *Winnipeg Free Press* read: "Henry R. Halpin Dies; Historic Link Broken." The news item surveyed his past history with the Hudson's Bay Company and Indian Affairs, noting that he was "one of the best acquainted with Indian tradition and legend in the west."[20]

His time on the frontiers of civilization in Western Canada had been a great adventure. His initial goal to live with the Indians, when he came to Fort Garry, had been realized, more than he would have ever imagined. He became a fur trader, he was held a prisoner by Native rebels in 1885, and then became an Indian agent. He had served as an interpreter for the Cree at Fort Pitt and Moose Mountain. He had not been a decision-maker in the Department of Indian Affairs, but played an important role in Native affairs at Moose Mountain. He had even married a "prairie flower" — Flora. As he looked over his life about 1927, while writing his longer manuscript, Halpin reflected, "in the twilight of life, I can look backward and have no regrets."

Henry Ross Halpin, circa *1928.*

Courtesy of Saskatchewan Archives Board, R-B821

Notes

Editor's Preface

1. The Northwest, or Riel, Rebellion was the result of the combination of long-standing complaints from starving Natives dispossessed of their traditional hunting grounds, landless English and French Métis, and angry white settlers in Saskatchewan protesting lack of action by the federal government and expressing their own desire for provincehood. Encouraged by the defeat of the North West Mounted Police (NWMP) at Duck Lake in March 1885, angry young Natives joined the rebellion with a hope of driving out the federal government and its agents. The multiple murders of whites at Frog Lake by rebel Cree struck terror in the hearts of western settlers. After federal troops suppressed the rebellion, Riel and a number of Natives were arrested and tried. Most were convicted and hanged for their activities.

2. Hellmuth College was founded by I. Hellmuth, later Anglican Bishop of Huron, in 1865. It was first known as London's Collegiate Institute. See The *London Advertiser*, September 8, 1882.

3. J.R.C. Honeyman's notation on the back of the Halpin typescript R-E2989, Saskatchewan Archives Board, dated October 27, 1922.

4. H.R. Halpin, "Forty-Five Aprils Ago I Was Big Bear's Captive," in *Manitoba Free Press*, 12 April 1930, 34.

5. See Stuart Hughes, ed., "The Frog Lake 'Massacre': Personal Perspectives on Ethnic Conflict" (Toronto: McClelland & Stewart, 1976). Father Le Goff referred to Halpin, but did not give his name.

6. See Sarah Carter, ed., *Two Months in the Camp of Big Bear: The Life and Adventures of Theresa Gowanlock and Theresa Delaney* (Regina: Canadian Plains Research Center, 1999), introduction.

7. The underlying ideology of the Indian Act has been described as overtly racist. For a full discussion, see James S. Frideres, *Native Peoples in Canada: Contemporary Conflicts*, 2nd ed. (Scarborough, ON: Prentice Hall Inc., 1983).

CHAPTER 1: FORT GARRY

1. A newspaper article, "Fort Alexander H.B. Agent Here," published in the *Manitoba Free Press*, December 14, 1905, 14, claimed that Halpin had first visited Red River in 1871 when he visited his uncle Bernard Rogan Ross at Lower Fort Garry. This contradicts another article, "Progress March Evokes Memories," in the *Manitoba Free Press*, October 19, 1929, 1, which stated that Halpin first visited Winnipeg in 1872. Halpin's own comments in this memoir suggest that he had already become an apprentice postmaster with the Hudson's Bay Company (HBC) before coming to Fort Garry. One HBC document (B.235/g/2, fo.8) gave his home as Montreal. He may have actually joined the Company in Montreal and trained there.

2. Apparently Blanket Indians were those whose main clothing consisted of blankets rather than the traditional animal skins and furs. The Hudson's Bay Company did a brisk trade in selling blankets to the Native Peoples.

3. Halpin's friend was probably Alexandre Hamelin.

4. See the 1901 Canada Census for Lac La Biche, T-6551, E2, 1, for Alexandre Hamelin. The birthplace of some of his children shows that he was living at Lac La Biche in 1880. During the Riel Rebellion in 1885 he was still living at Lac La Biche and was approached by the Plains Cree to join Riel, but he refused.

5. All Native People had to obtain permission from the Indian agent to go off the reserve and to transact any business. Indian agents controlled much of the lives of the Natives up until the 1960s.

6. Thomas Scott, an Irish-Protestant settler, had resisted Louis Riel's activities in Manitoba in 1870. After making death threats against Riel, Scott was court-martialled and executed on Riel's orders.

7. The "Minnesota Massacre" was also known as the Dakota War or the Sioux Uprising. In 1862, because of broken treaties, the Sioux attempted to drive white settlers out of Minnesota by attacking settlements. The American army was sent in to put down the uprising. Besides those Sioux killed in battle, thirty-eight were executed in a mass hanging.

8. The General Hospital that Halpin mentions appears to have evolved into today's Health Services Centre in Winnipeg.

9. See *The Manitoban*, 27 July 1872, 2 and 3 August 1872, 2, for coverage of the Reverend Punshon's visit to Winnipeg.

CHAPTER 2: LAKE WINNIPEG, A YORK BOAT, AND AN OX

1. The matter of Halpin having a servant is unclear. Halpin, himself, would have been regarded as a servant of the Company. For his rank, he is not likely to have been assigned an assistant. He may have been

referring to a Native hanger-on who helped him. Regardless, the issue speaks to Halpin's attitude of self-importance.

2. Here the manuscript is unclear. It continues Halpin's aside about an opportunity he had to acquire a quarter section of land at Victoria Beach for three sacks of flour in about 1903.

3. Hudson's Bay Company Archives [henceforth HBC Archives], Reel No. 1M1014, Norway House Journal, August 20, 1872, recorded Halpin's arrival.

CHAPTER 3: NORWAY HOUSE

1. Sir John Franklin's Royal Navy exploration party was last seen in 1845. Many expeditions were sent to find Franklin and his men between 1848 and 1859, but they only turned up some artifacts. It is now known from a journal that was found that Franklin's ships became trapped in the ice. An attempt was made to head south overland, but the crew members died of starvation and exposure. It is also believed, based on the bodies that were found (and recently exhumed and autopsied by archaeologists and pathologists at the University of Alberta) that the crew members suffered from lead poisoning contracted from the canned meat that had been taken with them as part of the food supplies.

2. Halpin was referring to the Reverend Egerton R. Young.

3. See Chapter One's discussion of Punshon's talk at Fort Garry.

4. HBC Archives, Film No. 1M1014, Norway House Journal, April 2, 1873, refers to Halpin's new assignment.

CHAPTER 4: NATIVE MYSTERIES AT NELSON RIVER POST

1. HBC Archives, Reel No. 1M1014, Norway House Journal, July 13, 1873.

2. Let us not forget the prize fights.

3. HBC Archives, Reel No. 1M1014, Norway House Journal, January 3, 1874, indicates that Halpin left for Nelson River Post on that day, not in March.

CHAPTER 5: STRANDED ON CROSS LAKE

1. HBC Archives, Reel No. 1M1014, Norway House Journal, June 9, 1874. Since Halpin arrived back at Norway House on June 9, 1874, it was probably in late May that this happened.

2. James Settee, a descendant of a Hudson's Bay Company official and a Swampy Cree woman, was one of the first Natives ordained by the Anglican Church in Rupert's Land. He worked as a missionary and schoolteacher among the Natives in present-day Saskatchewan and Manitoba for almost sixty years, trying to help them adapt to the changing economy as the fur trade was declining in importance. He died in Winnipeg in 1902.

3. Early Hudson's Bay Company and Royal Navy explorers mentioned Painted Stone with its pictographs on the Hayes River system. The site was regarded as sacred and Native ceremonies were held there. Local geographic features were known as Painted Stone Portage and Painted Stone River. According to Edward Chappell, whose Narrative was published in 1817, the pictographs at Painted Stone Portage had already disappeared (see page 192). Halpin appears to be describing other pictographs discovered where Cross Lake and Little Cross Lake join. He would have been following the Nelson River system.

It has not been possible to find any other discussion matching his descriptions of the pictographs, and they too may have disappeared over time or been deliberately destroyed by vandals, as was the case with other pictographs in the area.

4. HBC Archives, File D38/6a, 18 (stamped).

CHAPTER 6: OXFORD HOUSE

1. Halpin probably left Norway House on October 4, 1874. Journals kept for Norway House and Oxford House for that part of 1874 have not survived, but on October 3, 1875, Halpin mentioned his first anniversary of leaving Norway House being the following day. See HBC Archives, Reel No. 1M1017, Oxford House Journal, October 3, 1875.

2. Halpin appears to have employed some dramatic licence here. The Norway House Journal for August 20, 1872, shows that Halpin and Sinclair had arrived at Norway House with the same fleet of York boats that had come from Fort Garry. During Halpin's two years at Norway House, Sinclair was a frequent visitor to Norway House. Halpin also seems to have been up to Oxford House in 1873, and has conflated the events.

3. Halpin had spelled his name Germain. George H. Cornish, *Cyclopedia of Methodism in Canada* (Toronto: Methodist Book and Publishing House, 1881) spelled his name German.

4. Lord Selkirk, who had bought into the Hudson's Bay Company, had created humanitarian settlements for Scottish Highlanders in various parts of British North America: the Belfast settlement in Prince Edward Island, the Baldoon settlement in Upper Canada, and the Red River settlement in what became Manitoba. His creation of the Red River Colony in 1812 near Fort Garry led to an armed battle with the North West Company in 1816. The ongoing "fight" between the two companies led to the HBC acquiring the NWC in 1821 after Lord Selkirk's death. For more information on Selkirk, see Lucille H. Campey, *The Silver Chief: Lord Selkirk and the Scottish Pioneers of Belfast, Baldoon and Red River* (Toronto: Natural Heritage Books, 2001).

5. This probably happened at Christmas 1874. The Oxford House Journal for 1874 has not survived so we cannot be certain. Savoyard was mentioned in the Oxford House Journal by Halpin on August 27–28, 1875. See HBC Archives, film No. 1M1017.

Chapter 7: The Legends of God's Lake

1. When Halpin spoke about the bad (evil) men from Red River, he was likely referring to earlier North West Company men or free-traders who were cutting into the Hudson's Bay Company domain. Whether they had deliberately brought the disease into the area of God's Lake is a matter of question. It may have been inadvertent. Having no resistance to the disease, Native Peoples in western Canada were decimated by measles and smallpox, which had come up from the United States by way of the fur trade in the 1780s. Again, in 1837, a ship belonging to the American Fur Trade Company had carried smallpox into the Canadian plains.

Historically, smallpox had been used as a means of germ warfare in 1763 by the British Army to defeat Natives who were helping the French forces, by giving them smallpox-infected blankets. There are reports of renegade fur traders using the same tactics to kill off Natives and get their furs without having to purchase them. For a full discussion of the impact of smallpox, see Arthur J. Ray, *Indians in the Fur Trade: Their Role as Hunters, Trappers and Middlemen in the Lands Southwest of Hudson Bay, 1660–1870* (Toronto: University of Toronto Press, 1974), note index.

Chapter 8: York Factory

1. Halpin has described his time at York Factory as the winter of 1876–77, but his timeline does not square with the records. His memory of the dates may have been confused, but his impressions and experiences at York Factory are worth noting.

2. HBC Archives, Reel No. 1MB86, Oxford House Correspondence

(B.156/c/2), J. Fortescue to C. Sinclair, February 10, 1875.

3. HBC Archives, Reel No. 3M182, Oxford House Correspondence, C. Sinclair to Roderick Ross, February 19, 1875.

4. HBC Archives, Reel No. 1MB86, Oxford House Correspondence, Roderick Ross to C. Sinclair, February 27, 1875.

5. Not only the season, but the year appears incorrect.

6. That number of employees does not jibe with York Factory records. Halpin's figure may have included the Homeguard Cree, who provided casual labour.

7. Most of the English-speaking Métis had their roots in the Orkney Islands of Scotland, for more information on the Orkney men, see Lucille H. Campey, *An Unstoppable Force: The Scottish Exodus to Canada* (Toronto: Natural Heritage Books/The Dundurn Group, 2008), 98–100, 105–08.

8. Other sources put it about five miles away.

9. More accurately, the spring.

10. Halpin was not there during the winter of 1876–77. He may have been reporting hearsay or he meant the winter of 1874–75. Even then, he does not appear to have spent a Christmas at York Factory.

11. He had left York Factory at the end of June 1875.

12. Unfortunately, the York Factory Journal (Reel No. 1M1027) made no mention of this adventure. That is not surprising for the journal contained few details and Halpin's name was never mentioned during the time that he worked there although the correspondence does.

13. HBC Archives, Reel No. 1MB86, Oxford House Correspondence, (B.1566/c/2), J. Fortescue to C. Sinclair, June 10, 1875.

14. *Ibid.*, J. Fortescue to C. Sinclair, June 28, 1875.

CHAPTER 9: POSTMASTER

1. HBC Archives, Reel No. 1MB86, Oxford House Correspondence, (B.156/c/2), J.A. Grahame to C. Sinclair, May 13, 1875.

2. HBC Archives, Reel No. 1M1266, Minutes of Council, 1875–77.

3. HBC Archives, Reel No. 1MB86, Oxford House Correspondence, (B. 156/c/2), J.A. Grahame to C. Sinclair, August 12, 1875.

4. HBC Archives, Reel No. 1M1017, Oxford House Journal.

5. "Debting" appears to have been the giving of food supplies and other items to the Natives in anticipation of furs they would bring in. We would use the term "credit." These transactions were recorded in the account books for each Native person.

CHAPTER 10: ISLAND LAKE POST

1. HBC Archives, Reel No. 3M199, Commissioner's Correspondence, H.R. Halpin to J. Wrigley, August 22,1885.

2. HBC Archives, Reel No. 3M184, Commissioner's Correspondence Inward, (D.20/5), C. Sinclair to J.A. Grahame, July 3, 1876.

3. *Ibid.*

4. *Ibid.*

5. HBC Archives, Reel No. 1M1017, Oxford House Journal, July 9, 1876.

6. *Ibid.*, July 29, 1876.

7. *Ibid.*, September 26–27, 1876.

8. HBC Archives, Reel No. 3M154, Commissioner's Correspondence, J.A. Grahame to C. Sinclair, December 12, 1876.

9. HBC Archives, Reel No. 3M184, Commissioner's Correspondence Inward, Cuthbert Sinclair to J.A. Grahame, December 17, 1876.

CHAPTER 11: OFF TO THE NORTHWEST

1. HBC Archives, Reel No. 3M184, Commissioner's Correspondence Inward, C. Sinclair to J.A. Grahame, December 17, 1876. See also Oxford House Journal, December 18, 1876, which noted the arrival of the York Factory Express.

2. Oxford House Journal, December 18–21, 1876.

3. HBC Archives, Reel No. 1M1014, Norway House Journal, December 24, 1876.

4. *Ibid.*, January 6, 1877.

5. HBC Archives, Reel No. 3M214, Commissioner's Inward Telegrams (D.20/71), J.H. McTavish to J.A. Grahame, January 23, 1877.

6. HBC Archives, Reel No. 3M154, Commissioner's Correspondence Outward, J.A. Grahame to J.H. McTavish, January 23, 1877.

7. HBC Archives, Reel No. 3M184, Commissioner's Correspondence Inward, C. Sinclair to J.A. Grahame, December 17, 1876.

8. HBC Archives, Reel No. 1MB86, Oxford House Correspondence, (B.156/c/2), J.H. McTavish to C. Sinclair, March 12, 1877.

9. *Ibid.*, G.S. McTavish to C. Sinclair, March 12, 1877.

10. *Ibid.*, J.A. Grahame to C. Sinclair, 23 May 1877.

11. HBC Archives, Reel No. 1M1266, Council Minutes, 1877, 144.

12. HBC Archives, Reel No. 1M1263, Abstracts of Servants' Accounts, 1876–1878 (B.235/g).

13. *London Free Press*, 7 October 1878, 1.

14. The *Dominion Churchman*, 17 October 1878, 502, reported on the funeral, but there was no mention of specific family members. Because the issues for the *London Free Press* around the time of funeral were not microfilmed, we do not have a local funeral report.

15. Canada Census, 1881, C–13286, Peace River, District 192, 1.

16. HBC Archives, Reel No. 3M199, Commissioner's Correspondence Inward, H.R. Halpin to J. Wrigley, August 22, 1885.

17. See Thomas Flanagan, *Louis "David" Riel: Prophet of the New World* (Toronto: University of Toronto Press, 1979). See also Thomas Flanagan ed., *The Diaries of Louis Riel* (Edmonton: Hurtig Publishing, 1976). Flanagan discounts Riel's mental illness, seeing him instead as a religious visionary. For a more balanced view of Riel, see Hartwell Bowsfield, ed., *Louis Riel: Selected Readings* (Toronto: Copp Clark Pitman Ltd., 1988), and George F.G. Stanley, *Louis Riel* (Toronto: McGraw-Hill Ryerson Limited, 1963).

CHAPTER 12: A PRISONER WITH BIG BEAR

1. Halpin's shorter manuscript has been augmented by his testimony during the Rebellion trials and a *Manitoba Morning Free Press* report of a talk he had given to a Methodist youth group in Regina in 1894, as well as interviews he gave and an account he wrote in 1930. Where I have insrted Halpin's reflections from the other sources, I have footnoted them.

2. Halpin's testimony, "The Queen vs. Big Bear, 1885," Canada, *Sessional Papers*, 1886, Vol. 13, 212 [henceforth Halpin testimony]. The ellipses in the text represent the questions and interruptions by lawyers.

3. Île-á-la-Crosse was in northern Saskatchewan between 55 and 60 degrees latitude. It was possible to reach it by the Beaver River system and it would not be unusual to send flour to a Hudson's Bay Company outpost. As he planned his escape, Halpin thought of going there. There was a reference to that flour in the HBC Archives, Reel No. 3M199, Commissioner's Correspondence Inward, (D.20/36), L. Clark to Joseph Wrigley, June 30, 1885.

4. Not all the white people had been killed. In addition to W.B. Cameron, James Simpson, Theresa Delaney, and Theresa Gowanlock had been spared.

5. "Captured by Indians: Interesting Reminiscence of the Riel Rebellion," *Manitoba Morning Free Press*, 8 May 1894, 7.

6. *Ibid.*

7. Indian Agent Thomas Quinn was especially disliked by the Natives because of his abuse of them.

8. Halpin may have overstated Blondin's gallantry; other evidence suggests that his motives in regard to Mrs. Gowanlock were less than honourable. See Theresa Delaney and Theresa Gowanlock's account, *Two Months in*

the Camp of Big Bear, ed. Sarah Carter (Regina: Plains Research Center, 1999; reprinted from 1885), 18, 39.

9. The Prince Albert Volunteers were an auxiliary force formed by the North West Mounted Police.

10. Halpin testimony, 215–17.

11. *Ibid.*, 216.

12. The manuscript says Frog Lake; the context suggests Onion Lake. The place had been torched several days before and the white inhabitants had fled to Fort Pitt.

13. Halpin called him captain, but his rank was inspector — Inspector Francis J. Dickens. He was the son of Charles Dickens, the English novelist.

14. According to North West Mounted Police Inspector Dickens, Indian Agent Thomas Quinn had ordered the North West Mounted Police out of the Frog Lake Settlement because their presence was inflaming the already angry Cree. The Frog Lake detachment went to join Dickens and his men at Fort Pitt, leaving behind some of their horses. These were the police horses that Lone Man and his group had with them when they seized Halpin at Cold Lake. Canada, *Sessional Papers*, 1886, Vol. 19, No. 6, Francis J. Dickens to the Commissioner of the North West Mounted Police, 78–80.

15. Published in Charles Pelham Mulvaney, *The History of the North-West Rebellion of 1885* (Toronto: A.H. Hovey and Co., 1885), 125–26.

16. The Battle of Cut Knife occurred on May 2, 1885, when a combined force of North West Mounted Police and Canadian militia, led by Colonel William Otter, launched an unlawful and unprovoked attack on Chief Poundmaker's Cree encampment about thirty miles west of Battleford. Up until that time, Poundmaker had been peaceful. During the attack the NWMP and the militia suffered heavy losses and had to retreat.

Poundmaker is recognized as having prevented a further slaughter of the retreating forces. News of Poundmaker's success gave courage to the Cree renegades near Fort Pitt. For a contemporary account, see Charles Pelham Mulvaney, *The History of the North-West Rebellion of 1885* (Toronto: A.H. Hovey and Co., 1885) 156–93.

17. *Manitoba Morning Free Press*, 8 May 1894, 7.

18. *Ibid.*

19. Thomas Bland Strange was a retired British Army officer who previously had served in India and had organized the Canadian artillery.

20. *Manitoba Morning Free Press*, 8 May 1894, 7.

21. Halpin testimony, 217.

22. *Brandon Weekly Mail*, 13 August 1885, 8.

23. Halpin testimony, 218. Simpson later denied this statement.

24. Halpin testimony, 217.

25. *Ibid.*, 217.

26. Provincial Archives of Manitoba, Riel Series, MG3 D1, No. 617, Judge Richardson's trial notes, 90.

27. Canada, *Sessional Papers*, 1886, Vol. 19, "War Claims Commission, Report No. 35," October 17, 1885, 126.

28. Library and Archives Canada (henceforth LAC), Reel No. T–13147, RG 15, D–II–1, Volume 462, File 122927.

CHAPTER 13: MUSCOWPETUNG, FORT PELLY, AND INDIAN AFFAIRS

1. HBC Archives, Reel No. 3M199, Commissioner's Correspondence Inward, Henry R. Halpin to J. Wrigley, August 22, 1885.

2. *Ibid.*

3. HBC Archives, Reel No. 3M199, Commissioner's Correspondence Inward, D.20/36, Henry R. Halpin to J. Wrigley, September 11, 1885.

4. HBC Archives, Reel No. 3M167, Commissioner's Correspondence, J. Wrigley to Henry Ross Halpin, September 15, 1885.

5. *Qu'Appelle Vidette*, 12 November 1885, 3.

6. *Regina Leader*, 7 January 1886, 4.

7. *Winnipeg Daily Times*, 22 April 1884, 8, and 12 May 1884, 8.

8. Canada, *Sessional Papers*, 1887, Vol. 5, Indian Affairs Department Employee Statistics, Section 2, 11.

9. George Bryce, *Holiday Rambles Between Winnipeg and Victoria* (Winnipeg: 1888), 52.

10. *Regina Leader*, 16 December 1890, 8. The "Messiah Craze" may have been the Ghost Dance that had millenarian overtones, and later led to the Battle of Wounded Knee in South Dakota in 1890.

11. LAC, Reel No. C–10141, Indian Affairs, RG 10, Vol. 3808, File 53584. Note that in this file are documents pertaining also to Herbert B. Halpin, a different Indian agent.

12. LAC, Reel No. C–10155, Indian Affairs, RG 10, Vol. 3877, File 91839–1, Superintendent General of Indian Affairs to Privy Council, July 21, 1892.

13. LAC, MG 29, E106, Hayter Reed Fonds, Personnel Files, Henry Ross Halpin to Hayter Reed, December 22, 1892.

14. *Ibid.*, Hayter Reed to H.R. Halpin, January 7, 1893.

15. *Ibid.*, Hayter Reed to the Honourable J. Mayne Daly, Minister of the Interior, March 10, 1893.

16. *Ibid.*

17. *Ibid.*, H.R. Halpin to Hayter Reed, March 21, 1893.

18. *Ibid.*, Annie M.D. Halpin to Hayter Reed, April 2, 1893.

19. *Ibid.*, H.R. Halpin to Hayter Reed, May 2, 1893.

20. *Ibid.*, H.R. Halpin to Hayter Reed, May 3, 1893.

21. *Ibid.*, Hayter Reed to H.R. Halpin, May 13, 1893.

22. *Ibid.*, H.R. Halpin to Hayter Reed, May 30, 1893.

23. *Ibid.*, H.R. Halpin to Hayter Reed, September 23, 1893.

24. *Ibid.*, W. Jones to Hayter Reed, September 20, 1893.

25. LAC, Reel No. C–10141, Indian Affairs, RG 10, Volume 3808, File 53,584, H.R. Halpin to Hayter Reed, undated, but arrived in Ottawa, October 25, 1893.

26. Canada, *Sessional Papers*, 1895, Vol. 9, Department of Indian Affairs Employee List, 8.

27. J.R.C. Honeyman's note on the back of Halpin's sixteen-page typescript, October 27, 1922, Saskatchewan Archives Board.

28. LAC, Reel No. C–10141, Indian Affairs, RG 10, Volume 3808, File 53,584, A.E. Forget to Hayter Reed, February 2, 1894.

29. *Ibid.*

30. *Ibid.*, Hayter Reed to A.E. Forget, February 15, 1894.

Chapter 14: Moose Mountain Agency

1. As the West was being settled, communities were established in areas where it was thought that the Canadian Pacific Railway (CPR) would place its stations. Much land speculation took place and the CPR deliberately changed its location of tracks and stations so that it would have more economic control. This happened at Selkirk, Battleford, and Calgary.

2. Canada, *Sessional Papers*, 1897, Vol. 11, Department of Indian Affairs, 186.

3. Canada, *Sessional Papers*, 1898, Vol. 11, Department of Indian Affairs Employee List, 171.

4. Canada, *Sessional Papers*, 1900, Vol. 11, Department of Indian Affairs Employment List, 169.

5. The government had removed authority from White Bear because he was not compliant.

6. Canada, *Sessional Papers*, 1898, Vol. 11, H.R. Halpin to the Superintendent General of Indian Affairs, July 1, 1897, 158–162.

7. Canada, *Sessional Papers*, 1899, Vol. 12, Henry Ross Halpin to Superintendent General of Indian Affairs, July 4, 1898, 151–153.

8. *Ibid.*, 188.

9. The Sun Dance, also known as the Thirst Dance or Hungry Dance, was connected with a revival of Native religion that Christian missionaries and the government had been trying to suppress. Often it involved self-torture as Native men were tethered to a dance pole with hooks stuck in their chests. The prohibition against the ceremony was dropped from the Indian Act in 1951.

10. Canada, *Sessional Papers*, 1900, Volume 11, Henry Ross Halpin, to the Superintendent General of Indian Affairs, Ottawa, July 3, 1899, 157–159.

11. Canada, *Sessional Papers*, 1901, Vol. 11, Henry Ross Halpin to Superintendent General of Indian Affairs, July 4, 1900, 165–166.

12. Death Certificate No. 374, Cannington West, North-West Territories, 1900.

13. Canada Census, 1901, Reel No. T-6431, Brandon, B-8, 5. Baby Annie was also enumerated in Henry Halpin's return for 1901. See Reel No. T-6554, Assiniboia East, Moose Mountain Agency, 10.

14. Treaty No. 4 was signed in 1874 setting up Indian reserves in what is part of southern Alberta, Saskatchewan, and Manitoba. In addition to annuities, shot, agricultural tools, and seed were to be given to each family. Each reserve was to have a school, and Native hunting, trapping, and fishing rights were to be respected. Only about half of the Native groups were represented at the signing and the treaty's validity was often questioned. For the changes in government policy see Sarah Carter, *Lost Harvests: Prairie Indian Reserve Farmers and Government Policy* (Montreal: McGill-Queen's University Press, 1990).

15. Stewart Raby, "Indian Land Surrenders in Southern Saskatchewan," in *Canadian Geographer*, Vol. 17, No. 1 (Spring 1973): 36–38.

16. Canada, *Sessional Papers*, 1902, Vol. 11, Henry Ross Halpin to

Superintendent General of Indian Affairs, July 1901, 160–62.

17. *Ibid.*, Report by Alexander McGibbon, September 16, 1901, 201.

18. *Ibid.*, 198.

19. See Sarah Carter, 168–170.

20. Canada, *Sessional Papers*, 1904, Vol. 11, W. Murison to the Superintendent General of Indian Affairs, 171–73.

CHAPTER 15: FORT ALEXANDER AND EPILOGUE

1. HBC Archives, D.38/57.

2. Saskatchewan Archives Board, Halpin File, Eva (Halpin) Lawrence to Z.M. Hamilton, Saskatchewan Historical Society, October 27, 1945.

3. HBC Archives, D.38/20, 61.

4. HBC Archives, Reel No. 1M1081, Lower Fort Garry Correspondence, J. Stauger to the Commissioner, October 10, 1903,

5. HBC Archives, Reel No. 1M1033, Fort Alexander Correspondence, H.R. Halpin to the Commissioner, November 23, 1903.

6. Canada, Prairie Census, 1906, Reel No. T-18356, Selkirk, Sub-Division 8, 5. An eighteen-year-old "Clance" Halpin was listed as a daughter. This appears to have been a mistake and Clance may have been a nickname for son Claude.

7. HBC Archives, Reel No. 1M1033, Fort Alexander Correspondence, H.R. Halpin to Post Office Inspector, July 11, 1904.

8. HBC Archives, D.38/20, 62.

9. "Fort Alexander H.B. Agent Here," in *Manitoba Free Press,* 14 February 1905, 14.

10. HBC Archives, D.38/57, 157.

11. LAC, Reel No. C–6600, Liber 828, folio 234; Canada, 1911 Census, Manitoba, Selkirk, 22, sub-division 27, 12.

12. For more on the Halpin Family, see a local history published in 1984 by the Rural Municipality of St. Clements, entitled *East Side of the Red, 1884-1984,* 578–80.

13. LAC, RG 150, Acc. 1992–93/166, Box 3965–16, military file for Jack Halpin.

14. LAC, RG 150, Acc. 1991–93/166, Box 3965–5, military file for Charles Bernard Halpin.

15. PAM, MG 12 J1, J.H. Meanwell to Henry R. Halpin, December 2, 1926.

16. "Progress March Evokes Memories," *Manitoba Free Press*, 19 October 1929, 1.

17. *Manitoba Morning Free Press*, 19 February 1900, 9.

18. Saskatchewan Archives Board, H.R. Halpin to Judge H.A. Robson, February 8, 1928, attached to longer Halpin manuscript.

19. H.R. Halpin, "Forty-Five Aprils Ago I Was Big Bear's Captive," *Manitoba Free Press*, 12 April 1930, 34. The title of this article was unfortunate because the contents show that Halpin was not Big Bear's captive.

20. *Winnipeg Free Press*, May 6, 1930, 1.

Bibliography

Archival Sources

Library and Archives Canada (LAC)
    Canada: Census, 1871–1911
    Canada: Department of Indian Affairs files
    Canada: Department of the Interior files
    Canada: *Sessional Papers*, 1885–1902
    Hayter Reed Fonds
    Hudson's Bay Company microfilms

Manitoba Archives and Hudson's Bay Company Archives
    Hudson's Bay Company documents
    H.R. Halpin personnel file
    Judge Hugh Richardson court notes *re* trial of Riel and others, MG
        3 D1, No. 671
    T.A. Burrows file, MG 12 J1, No. 15

Saskatchewan Archives Board
    Halpin's 16-page typescript and his 121-page manuscript, R-E2989

Glenbow-Alberta Institute Photographic Collection

BOOKS

Beal, Bob and Rod Macleod. *Prairie Fire: The 1885 North-West Rebellion.* Edmonton: Hurtig Books, 1984.

Begg, Alexander. *"Dot it Down:" A Story of a Life in the North-West.* Toronto: Junter, Rose, 1871.

Brown, Jennifer S.H. *Strangers in Blood: Fur Trade Company Families in Indian Country.* Vancouver: University of British Columbia Press, 1980.

Bryce, George. *Holiday Rambles Between Winnipeg and Victoria.* Winnipeg: self-published, 1888.

Butler, William Francis. *The Great Lone Land: A Narrative of Travel and Adventure.* London: S. Low, Marston, Searle and Revington, 1878.

Cameron, William Beasdell. *The War Trail of Big Bear.* Boston: Small Maynard and Co., 1927.

Campey, Lucille H. *The Silver Chief: Lord Selkirk and the Scottish Pioneers of Belfast, Baldoon and Red River.* Toronto: Natural Heritage Books, 2001.

_____. *An Unstoppable Force: The Scottish Exodus to Canada.* Toronto: Natural Heritage Books/Dundurn Press, 2008.

Carter, Sarah. *Lost Harvests: Prairie Indian Reserve Farmers and Government Policy.* Montreal: McGill-Queen's University Press, 1990.

_____, ed. *Two Months in the Camp of Big Bear: The Life and Adventures of Theresa Gowanlock and Theresa Delaney.* Regina: Canadian Plains Research Center, 1999.

Cowie, Issac. *The Company of Adventurers: A Narrative of Seven Years in the Service of the Hudson's Bay Company During 1867–1874, on the Great Buffalo Plains*. Toronto: W. Briggs, 1913.

Dempsey, Hugh A. *Big Bear: The End of Freedom*. Vancouver: Douglas and McIntyre, 1984.

Elliott, David R. "In Defense of Big Bear: The Role of Henry Ross Halpin," in *Prairie Forum*, Vol. 28, No. 1 (Spring 2003): 27–43.

Frideres, James S. *Native People in Canada: Contemporary Conflicts*, 2nd edition. Scarborough: Prentice Hall Canada Inc., 1983.

Friesen, Gerald. *The Canadian Prairies: A History*. Toronto: University of Toronto Press, 1984.

Grant, John Webster. *Moon of Wintertime: Missionaries and the Indians of Canada in Encounter since 1534*. Toronto: University of Toronto Press, 1984.

Hughes, Stuart, ed. *The Frog Lake "Massacre": Personal Perspectives on Ethnic Conflict*. Toronto: McClelland & Stewart, 1976.

Innis, Harold A. *The Fur Trade in Canada: An Introduction to Canadian Economic History*. Toronto: University of Toronto Press, 1930, revised 1956.

Macdonald, R.H., ed. *Eyewitness to History: William Bleasdell Cameron, Frontier Journalist*. Saskatoon: Western Producer Books, 1985.

Miller, J.R. *Big Bear (Mistahimusqua)*. Toronto: ECW Press, 1996.

_____. *Skyscrapers Hide the Heavens: A History of Indian-White Relations in Canada*, revised edition. Toronto: University of Toronto Press, 1991.

Moberly, Henry John with William Bleasdell Cameron. *When Fur Was King*. Toronto: J.M. Dent and Sons, Ltd., 1929.

Morton, Desmond, ed. *The Queen v Louis Riel*. Toronto: University of Toronto Press, 1974.

Mulvaney, Charles Pelham. *The History of the North-West Rebellion*. Toronto: A.H. Hovey and Co., 1885.

Newman, Peter C. *Merchant Princes*. Toronto: Penguin Books Canada Ltd., 1991.

Payne, Michael. *The Most Respectable Place in the Territory: Everyday Life in Hudson's Bay Company Service, York Factory, 1788–1870*. Ottawa: National Historic Parks and Sites, 1989.

Raby, Stewart. "Indian Land Surrenders in Southern Saskatchewan," in *Canadian Geographer*, Vol. 17, No. 1 (Spring 1973).

Ray, Arthur J. *The Canadian Fur Trade in the Industrial Age*. Toronto: University of Toronto Press, 1990.

_____. *Indians in the Fur Trade*. Toronto: University of Toronto Press, 1974.

_____ and Donald B. Freeman. *"Give Us Good Measure": An Economic Analysis of Relations between the Indians and the Hudson's Bay Company Before 1763*. Toronto: University of Toronto Press, 1978.

Rich, E.E. *The Fur Trade and the North-West to 1857*. Toronto: McClelland & Stewart, 1967.

Robinson, William M. *Novice in the North*. Surrey, BC: Hancock House, 1984.

Steele, Samuel Benfield. *Forty Years in Canada: Reminiscences of the Great North West*. London: H. Jenkins, Ltd., 1915.

Stonechild, Blair and Bill Waiser. *Loyal Till Death: Indians and the North-West Rebellion*. Calgary: Fifth House, 1997.

Talman, James J. *Huron College, 1863–1963*. London: Huron College, 1963.

Van Kirk, Sylvia. *"Many Tender Ties": Women in Fur-Trade Society, 1670–1870*. Winnipeg: Watson and Dwyer Publishing Ltd., 1980.

Weibe, Rudy and Bob Beale, eds. *War in the West: Voices of the 1885 Rebellion*. Toronto: McClelland & Stewart, 1985.

INDEX

ABOUT THE AUTHOR

*D*avid R. Elliott was born and raised in British Columbia. Later, at the University of Calgary, he earned his BA Honours in history and archaeology and an MA in western Canadian history. His PhD from the University of British Columbia focused on social and intellectual history. In addition, he holds a Master of Divinity degree from McMaster University. He has taught Canadian and European history at universities and colleges in British Columbia, Alberta, Ontario, and Nova Scotia, He is the co-author of *Bible Bill: A Biography of William Aberhart,* Alberta's controversial premier from 1935–43, and has edited a collection of Aberhart's writings and published many articles on Canadian political and religious history. Currently, he operates Kinfolk Finders, a historical and genealogical research company that specializes in Canadian and Irish genealogy.